CS-60 GENERAL APTITUDE AND ABILITIES SERIES

This is your PASSBOOK for...

Record Keeping

Test Preparation Study Guide Questions & Answers

NLC®
NATIONAL LEARNING CORPORATION®

National Learning Corporation

212 Michael Drive, Syosset, NY 11791
(516) 921-8888 • www.passbooks.com
E-mail: info@passbooks.com

PASSBOOK® SERIES

THE *PASSBOOK® SERIES* has been created to prepare applicants and candidates for the ultimate academic battlefield – the examination room.

At some time in our lives, each and every one of us may be required to take an examination – for validation, matriculation, admission, qualification, registration, certification, or licensure.

Based on the assumption that every applicant or candidate has met the basic formal educational standards, has taken the required number of courses, and read the necessary texts, the *PASSBOOK® SERIES* furnishes the one special preparation which may assure passing with confidence, instead of failing with insecurity. Examination questions – together with answers – are furnished as the basic vehicle for study so that the mysteries of the examination and its compounding difficulties may be eliminated or diminished by a sure method.

This book is meant to help you pass your examination provided that you qualify and are serious in your objective.

The entire field is reviewed through the huge store of content information which is succinctly presented through a provocative and challenging approach – the question-and-answer method.

A climate of success is established by furnishing the correct answers at the end of each test.

You soon learn to recognize types of questions, forms of questions, and patterns of questioning. You may even begin to anticipate expected outcomes.

You perceive that many questions are repeated or adapted so that you can gain acute insights, which may enable you to score many sure points.

You learn how to confront new questions, or types of questions, and to attack them confidently and work out the correct answers.

You note objectives and emphases, and recognize pitfalls and dangers, so that you may make positive educational adjustments.

Moreover, you are kept fully informed in relation to new concepts, methods, practices, and directions in the field.

You discover that you are actually taking the examination all the time: you are preparing for the examination by "taking" an examination, not by reading extraneous and/or supererogatory textbooks.

In short, this PASSBOOK®, used directedly, should be an important factor in helping you to pass your test.

OFFICE RECORD KEEPING

INTRODUCTION

This test guide provides a general description of the majority of the subject areas which will be tested and the different types of questions on the office record keeping test. While this test guide provides information on many of the subject areas in the office record keeping examinations, it may not provide information for all the subject areas in your examination.

OFFICE RECORD KEEPING

These questions test your ability to perform common office record keeping tasks. The test consists of two or more "sets" of questions, each set concerning a different problem. Typical record keeping problems might involve the organization or collation of data from several sources; scheduling; maintaining a record system using running balances; or completion of a table summarizing data using totals, subtotals, averages, and percents. There will be 15 questions in this subject area on the written test.

Test Tasks: The test consists of two or more "sets" of questions. Each set involves a different type of problem. Some examples of typical record keeping problems are:

- The organization or collation of data from several sources
- Scheduling
- Maintaining a record system using running balances
- completion of a table summarizing data using totals, subtotals, averages, and percents

NOTE: Only one type of problem set is presented in this test guide for this subject area. The actual test may or may not have a set of this type. It will certainly have at least one set involving a different type of problem.

On the following pages are two tables and three sample questions based on the tables. The solutions are at the end of this guide. Please look at the tables, and read both the questions and the solutions carefully.

- After each of the sample questions are four choices: for most questions, three choices are numbers and one choice is the statement "none of the above." For these questions, once you have completed your computations, select either the choice which is the same as your answer, or, if no choice matches your answer, select "none of the above."
- Some questions have numbers for all four choices. If none of the choices matches your calculation, you have made an error, and you should recheck your work.

DIRECTIONS FOR SAMPLE QUESTIONS: Base your answers to the next three sample questions on the table, "Summary Report of Business Expenses for 2014." Complete as much of the report as you need to answer the sample questions. Use the information given in the summary report itself and in the table, "Report of Business Expenses, 3rd and 4th Quarters."

REPORT OF BUSINESS EXPENSES 3RD AND 4TH QUARTERS (26 WEEKS)				
	3RD Quarter		4th Quarter	
	2014	2013	2014	2013
Payroll Expenses	$55,900	$47,800	$72,700	$65,100
Rental Expenses	22,500	18,900	22,500	18,900
Equipment Expenses				
New Equipment	705	375	5,575	675
Maintenance/Repair	2,860	3,000	3,140	3,400
Utility Expenses				
Electricity	4,850	4,630	4,590	4,450
Heat	130	270	440	410
Employee Benefit Expenses	18,450	15,850	24,100	21,550
Employee Contributions	*2,500	*2,200	*3,350	*3,040
Total Net Business Expenses*		$88,625		$111,445
*NOTE: Employee Contributions are subtracted from business expenses to obtain Total Net Business Expenses				

SUMMARY REPORT OF BUSINESS EXPENSES FOR 2014							
	1st Quarter	2nd Quarter	1st Half	3rd Quarter	4th Quarter	2nd Half	Total For Year
Payroll Expenses	$81,800	$69,300	$151,100			R	
Rental Expenses	22,500	22,500	45,000				
Equipment Expenses	5,235	3,545	8,780				S
Utility Expenses	6,675	5,125	11,800				
Employee Benefit Expenses	26,900	22,900	49,800				
Employee Contributions	*3,750	*3,200	*6,950				
Total Net Business Expenses* for 2014	139,360	120,170	259,530				
Total Net Business Expenses* for 2013			$231,780			$200,070	
% Change**			V				
*NOTE: Employee Contributions are subtracted from business expenses to obtain Total Net Business Expenses							
**NOTE: % Change is the % of increase in Total Net Business Expenses from 2013 to 2014							

1. What is the value of R? 1.____
   A. $112,900
   B. $128,600
   C. $137,800
   D. None of the above

2. What is the value of S? 2.____
   A. $8,780 B. $15,060
   C. $16,230 D. None of the above

3. Which one of the following is CLOSEST to the value of V? 3.____
   A. 10% B. 11% C. 12% D. 28%

KEY (CORRECT ANSWERS)

1. The correct answer is B. To answer this question correctly you must calculate the value of R (the Payroll Expenses for the 2nd Half of 2014).
   The Payroll Expenses for the 3rd and 4th Quarters are shown in the table, "Report of Business Expenses 3rd and 4th Quarters." (Be careful to use the amounts for 2014, and not the amounts for 2013.)
   You must add the Payroll Expenses for the 3rd Quarter of 2014 ($55,900) to the Payroll Expenses for the 4th Quarter of 2014 ($72,700).
   The result is $128,600, which is choice B.

2. The correct answer is D. To answer this question correctly, you must calculate the value of S (the Total Equipment Expenses for the year 2014).
   - You need to understand that Equipment Expenses are expenses for both New Equipment and for Maintenance/Repair.
   - The Equipment Expenses for the 3rd and 4th Quarters are shown in the table, "Report of Business Expenses 3rd and 4th Quarters." (Again, be careful to use the amounts for 2014, and not the amounts for 2013.)
   - You must add the Equipment Expenses for the 3rd Quarter of 2014 ($705 + $2,860) to Equipment Expenses for the 4th Quarter of 2014 ($5,575 + $3,140) in order to calculate Equipment Expenses for the 2nd Half of 2014.
   - $705 + $2,860 + $5,575 + $3,140 = $12,280.
   - You must then add Equipment Expenses for the 2nd half of 2014 to Equipment Expenses for the 1st half of 2014, in order to calculate Equipment Expenses for the whole year.
   - Equipment Expenses for the 1st half of 2014 are shown in the table, "Summary Report of Business Expenses for 2014."
   - $12,280 + $8,780 = $21,060. This is the value of S, the Total Equipment Expenses for the year 2014. Since none of A, B, or C choices is $21,060, the correct answer is "None of the above."

3. The correct answer is C (12%). To answer this question correctly, you must calculate the value of V (the percent change in Total Net Business Expenses from the first half of 2013 to the 1st half of 2014.

- You must first calculate the amount of change in Total Net Business Expenses from the 1st half of 2013 to the 1st half of 2014.
- Subtract the Total Net Business Expenses for the 1st half of 2013 ($231,780) from the Total Net Business Expenses for the 1st half of 2014 ($259,530).
- The result is $27,750.
- You must then calculate the percent change from the 1st half of 2013 to the 1st half of 2014. Since the percent change is from the 1st half of 2013, the basis of the comparison is the Total Net Business Expenses for the 1st half of 2013.
- Divide the amount of the change by the Total Net Business Expenses for the 1st half of 2013.
- $27,750 divided by $231,780 = .119726, or 11.9726%.
- This is closest to 12% (choice C).

HOW TO TAKE A TEST

You have studied long, hard and conscientiously.

With your official admission card in hand, and your heart pounding, you have been admitted to the examination room.

You note that there are several hundred other applicants in the examination room waiting to take the same test.

They all appear to be equally well prepared.

You know that nothing but your best effort will suffice. The "moment of truth" is at hand: you now have to demonstrate objectively, in writing, your knowledge of content and your understanding of subject matter.

You are fighting the most important battle of your life—to pass and/or score high on an examination which will determine your career and provide the economic basis for your livelihood.

What extra, special things should you know and should you do in taking the examination?

I. YOU MUST PASS AN EXAMINATION

A. WHAT EVERY CANDIDATE SHOULD KNOW

Examination applicants often ask us for help in preparing for the written test. What can I study in advance? What kinds of questions will be asked? How will the test be given? How will the papers be graded?

B. HOW ARE EXAMS DEVELOPED?

Examinations are carefully written by trained technicians who are specialists in the field known as "psychological measurement," in consultation with recognized authorities in the field of work that the test will cover. These experts recommend the subject matter areas or skills to be tested; only those knowledges or skills important to your success on the job are included. The most reliable books and source materials available are used as references. Together, the experts and technicians judge the difficulty level of the questions.

Test technicians know how to phrase questions so that the problem is clearly stated. Their ethics do not permit "trick" or "catch" questions. Questions may have been tried out on sample groups, or subjected to statistical analysis, to determine their usefulness.

Written tests are often used in combination with performance tests, ratings of training and experience, and oral interviews. All of these measures combine to form the best-known means of finding the right person for the right job.

II. HOW TO PASS THE WRITTEN TEST

A. BASIC STEPS

1) Study the announcement

How, then, can you know what subjects to study? Our best answer is: "Learn as much as possible about the class of positions for which you've applied." The exam will test the knowledge, skills and abilities needed to do the work.

Your most valuable source of information about the position you want is the official exam announcement. This announcement lists the training and experience qualifications. Check these standards and apply only if you come reasonably close to meeting them. Many jurisdictions preview the written test in the exam announcement by including a section called "Knowledge and Abilities Required," "Scope of the Examination," or some similar heading. Here you will find out specifically what fields will be tested.

2) Choose appropriate study materials

If the position for which you are applying is technical or advanced, you will read more advanced, specialized material. If you are already familiar with the basic principles of your field, elementary textbooks would waste your time. Concentrate on advanced textbooks and technical periodicals. Think through the concepts and review difficult problems in your field.

These are all general sources. You can get more ideas on your own initiative, following these leads. For example, training manuals and publications of the government agency which employs workers in your field can be useful, particularly for technical and professional positions. A letter or visit to the government department involved may result in more specific study suggestions, and certainly will provide you with a more definite idea of the exact nature of the position you are seeking.

3) Study this book!

III. KINDS OF TESTS

Tests are used for purposes other than measuring knowledge and ability to perform specified duties. For some positions, it is equally important to test ability to make adjustments to new situations or to profit from training. In others, basic mental abilities not dependent on information are essential. Questions which test these things may not appear as pertinent to the duties of the position as those which test for knowledge and information. Yet they are often highly important parts of a fair examination. For very general questions, it is almost impossible to help you direct your study efforts. What we can do is to point out some of the more common of these general abilities needed in public service positions and describe some typical questions.

1) General information

Broad, general information has been found useful for predicting job success in some kinds of work. This is tested in a variety of ways, from vocabulary lists to questions about current events. Basic background in some field of work, such as sociology or economics, may be sampled in a group of questions. Often these are principles which have become familiar to most persons through exposure rather than through formal training. It is difficult to advise you how to study for these questions; being alert to the world around you is our best suggestion.

2) Verbal ability

An example of an ability needed in many positions is verbal or language ability. Verbal ability is, in brief, the ability to use and understand words. Vocabulary and grammar tests are typical measures of this ability. Reading comprehension or paragraph interpretation questions are common in many kinds of civil service tests. You are given a paragraph of written material and asked to find its central meaning.

IV. KINDS OF QUESTIONS

1. Multiple-choice Questions

Most popular of the short-answer questions is the "multiple choice" or "best answer" question. It can be used, for example, to test for factual knowledge, ability to solve problems or judgment in meeting situations found at work.

A multiple-choice question is normally one of three types:

- It can begin with an incomplete statement followed by several possible endings. You are to find the one ending which best completes the statement, although some of the others may not be entirely wrong.
- It can also be a complete statement in the form of a question which is answered by choosing one of the statements listed.
- It can be in the form of a problem – again you select the best answer.

Here is an example of a multiple-choice question with a discussion which should give you some clues as to the method for choosing the right answer:

When an employee has a complaint about his assignment, the action which will best help him overcome his difficulty is to

A. discuss his difficulty with his coworkers
B. take the problem to the head of the organization
C. take the problem to the person who gave him the assignment
D. say nothing to anyone about his complaint

In answering this question, you should study each of the choices to find which is best. Consider choice "A" – Certainly an employee may discuss his complaint with fellow employees, but no change or improvement can result, and the complaint remains unresolved. Choice "B" is a poor choice since the head of the organization probably does not know what assignment you have been given, and taking your problem to him is known as "going over the head" of the supervisor. The supervisor, or person who made the assignment, is the person who can clarify it or correct any injustice. Choice "C" is, therefore, correct. To say nothing, as in choice "D," is unwise. Supervisors have and interest in knowing the problems employees are facing, and the employee is seeking a solution to his problem.

2. True/False

3. Matching Questions

Matching an answer from a column of choices within another column.

V. RECORDING YOUR ANSWERS

Computer terminals are used more and more today for many different kinds of exams.

For an examination with very few applicants, you may be told to record your answers in the test booklet itself. Separate answer sheets are much more common. If this separate answer sheet is to be scored by machine – and this is often the case – it is highly important that you mark your answers correctly in order to get credit.

VI. BEFORE THE TEST

YOUR PHYSICAL CONDITION IS IMPORTANT

If you are not well, you can't do your best work on tests. If you are half asleep, you can't do your best either. Here are some tips:

1) Get about the same amount of sleep you usually get. Don't stay up all night before the test, either partying or worrying—DON'T DO IT!
2) If you wear glasses, be sure to wear them when you go to take the test. This goes for hearing aids, too.
3) If you have any physical problems that may keep you from doing your best, be sure to tell the person giving the test. If you are sick or in poor health, you relay cannot do your best on any test. You can always come back and take the test some other time.

Common sense will help you find procedures to follow to get ready for an examination. Too many of us, however, overlook these sensible measures. Indeed, nervousness and fatigue have been found to be the most serious reasons why applicants fail to do their best on civil service tests. Here is a list of reminders:

- Begin your preparation early – Don't wait until the last minute to go scurrying around for books and materials or to find out what the position is all about.
- Prepare continuously – An hour a night for a week is better than an all-night cram session. This has been definitely established. What is more, a night a week for a month will return better dividends than crowding your study into a shorter period of time.
- Locate the place of the exam – You have been sent a notice telling you when and where to report for the examination. If the location is in a different town or otherwise unfamiliar to you, it would be well to inquire the best route and learn something about the building.
- Relax the night before the test – Allow your mind to rest. Do not study at all that night. Plan some mild recreation or diversion; then go to bed early and get a good night's sleep.
- Get up early enough to make a leisurely trip to the place for the test – This way unforeseen events, traffic snarls, unfamiliar buildings, etc. will not upset you.
- Dress comfortably – A written test is not a fashion show. You will be known by number and not by name, so wear something comfortable.
- Leave excess paraphernalia at home – Shopping bags and odd bundles will get in your way. You need bring only the items mentioned in the official notice you received; usually everything you need is provided. Do not bring reference books to the exam. They will only confuse those last minutes and be taken away from you when in the test room.

- Arrive somewhat ahead of time – If because of transportation schedules you must get there very early, bring a newspaper or magazine to take your mind off yourself while waiting.
- Locate the examination room – When you have found the proper room, you will be directed to the seat or part of the room where you will sit. Sometimes you are given a sheet of instructions to read while you are waiting. Do not fill out any forms until you are told to do so; just read them and be prepared.
- Relax and prepare to listen to the instructions
- If you have any physical problem that may keep you from doing your best, be sure to tell the test administrator. If you are sick or in poor health, you really cannot do your best on the exam. You can come back and take the test some other time.

VII. AT THE TEST

The day of the test is here and you have the test booklet in your hand. The temptation to get going is very strong. Caution! There is more to success than knowing the right answers. You must know how to identify your papers and understand variations in the type of short-answer question used in this particular examination. Follow these suggestions for maximum results from your efforts:

1) Cooperate with the monitor

The test administrator has a duty to create a situation in which you can be as much at ease as possible. He will give instructions, tell you when to begin, check to see that you are marking your answer sheet correctly, and so on. He is not there to guard you, although he will see that your competitors do not take unfair advantage. He wants to help you do your best.

2) Listen to all instructions

Don't jump the gun! Wait until you understand all directions. In most civil service tests you get more time than you need to answer the questions. So don't be in a hurry. Read each word of instructions until you clearly understand the meaning. Study the examples, listen to all announcements and follow directions. Ask questions if you do not understand what to do.

3) Identify your papers

Civil service exams are usually identified by number only. You will be assigned a number; you must not put your name on your test papers. Be sure to copy your number correctly. Since more than one exam may be given, copy your exact examination title.

4) Plan your time

Unless you are told that a test is a "speed" or "rate of work" test, speed itself is usually not important. Time enough to answer all the questions will be provided, but this does not mean that you have all day. An overall time limit has been set. Divide the total time (in minutes) by the number of questions to determine the approximate time you have for each question.

5) Do not linger over difficult questions

If you come across a difficult question, mark it with a paper clip (useful to have along) and come back to it when you have been through the booklet. One caution if you do this – be sure to skip a number on your answer sheet as well. Check often to be sure that you have not lost your place and that you are marking in the row numbered the same as the question you are answering.

6) Read the questions

Be sure you know what the question asks! Many capable people are unsuccessful because they failed to read the questions correctly.

7) Answer all questions

Unless you have been instructed that a penalty will be deducted for incorrect answers, it is better to guess than to omit a question.

8) Speed tests

It is often better NOT to guess on speed tests. It has been found that on timed tests people are tempted to spend the last few seconds before time is called in marking answers at random – without even reading them – in the hope of picking up a few extra points. To discourage this practice, the instructions may warn you that your score will be "corrected" for guessing. That is, a penalty will be applied. The incorrect answers will be deducted from the correct ones, or some other penalty formula will be used.

9) Review your answers

If you finish before time is called, go back to the questions you guessed or omitted to give them further thought. Review other answers if you have time.

10) Return your test materials

If you are ready to leave before others have finished or time is called, take ALL your materials to the monitor and leave quietly. Never take any test material with you. The monitor can discover whose papers are not complete, and taking a test booklet may be grounds for disqualification.

VIII. EXAMINATION TECHNIQUES

1) Read the general instructions carefully. These are usually printed on the first page of the exam booklet. As a rule, these instructions refer to the timing of the examination; the fact that you should not start work until the signal and must stop work at a signal, etc. If there are any special instructions, such as a choice of questions to be answered, make sure that you note this instruction carefully.

2) When you are ready to start work on the examination, that is as soon as the signal has been given, read the instructions to each question booklet, underline any key words or phrases, such as least, best, outline, describe and the like. In this way you will tend to answer as requested rather than discover on reviewing your paper that you listed without describing, that you selected the worst choice rather than the best choice, etc.

3) If the examination is of the objective or multiple-choice type – that is, each question will also give a series of possible answers: A, B, C or D, and you are called upon to select the best answer and write the letter next to that answer on your answer paper – it is advisable to start answering each question in turn. There may be anywhere from 50 to 100 such questions in the three or four hours allotted and you can see how much time would be taken if you read through all the questions before beginning to answer any. Furthermore, if you

come across a question or group of questions which you know would be difficult to answer, it would undoubtedly affect your handling of all the other questions.

4) If the examination is of the essay type and contains but a few questions, it is a moot point as to whether you should read all the questions before starting to answer any one. Of course, if you are given a choice – say five out of seven and the like – then it is essential to read all the questions so you can eliminate the two that are most difficult. If, however, you are asked to answer all the questions, there may be danger in trying to answer the easiest one first because you may find that you will spend too much time on it. The best technique is to answer the first question, then proceed to the second, etc.

5) Time your answers. Before the exam begins, write down the time it started, then add the time allowed for the examination and write down the time it must be completed, then divide the time available somewhat as follows:
   - If 3-1/2 hours are allowed, that would be 210 minutes. If you have 80 objective-type questions, that would be an average of 2-1/2 minutes per question. Allow yourself no more than 2 minutes per question, or a total of 160 minutes, which will permit about 50 minutes to review.
   - If for the time allotment of 210 minutes there are 7 essay questions to answer, that would average about 30 minutes a question. Give yourself only 25 minutes per question so that you have about 35 minutes to review.

6) The most important instruction is to read each question and make sure you know what is wanted. The second most important instruction is to time yourself properly so that you answer every question. The third most important instruction is to answer every question. Guess if you have to but include something for each question. Remember that you will receive no credit for a blank and will probably receive some credit if you write something in answer to an essay question. If you guess a letter – say "B" for a multiple-choice question – you may have guessed right. If you leave a blank as an answer to a multiple-choice question, the examiners may respect your feelings but it will not add a point to your score. Some exams may penalize you for wrong answers, so in such cases only, you may not want to guess unless you have some basis for your answer.

7) Suggestions
   a. Objective-type questions
      1. Examine the question booklet for proper sequence of pages and questions
      2. Read all instructions carefully
      3. Skip any question which seems too difficult; return to it after all other questions have been answered
      4. Apportion your time properly; do not spend too much time on any single question or group of questions
      5. Note and underline key words – all, most, fewest, least, best, worst, same, opposite, etc.
      6. Pay particular attention to negatives
      7. Note unusual option, e.g., unduly long, short, complex, different or similar in content to the body of the question
      8. Observe the use of "hedging" words – probably, may, most likely, etc.

9. Make sure that your answer is put next to the same number as the question
10. Do not second-guess unless you have good reason to believe the second answer is definitely more correct
11. Cross out original answer if you decide another answer is more accurate; do not erase until you are ready to hand your paper in
12. Answer all questions; guess unless instructed otherwise
13. Leave time for review

b. Essay questions
   1. Read each question carefully
   2. Determine exactly what is wanted. Underline key words or phrases.
   3. Decide on outline or paragraph answer
   4. Include many different points and elements unless asked to develop any one or two points or elements
   5. Show impartiality by giving pros and cons unless directed to select one side only
   6. Make and write down any assumptions you find necessary to answer the questions
   7. Watch your English, grammar, punctuation and choice of words
   8. Time your answers; don't crowd material

8) Answering the essay question

Most essay questions can be answered by framing the specific response around several key words or ideas. Here are a few such key words or ideas:

M's: manpower, materials, methods, money, management
P's: purpose, program, policy, plan, procedure, practice, problems, pitfalls, personnel, public relations

a. Six basic steps in handling problems:
   1. Preliminary plan and background development
   2. Collect information, data and facts
   3. Analyze and interpret information, data and facts
   4. Analyze and develop solutions as well as make recommendations
   5. Prepare report and sell recommendations
   6. Install recommendations and follow up effectiveness

b. Pitfalls to avoid
   1. Taking things for granted – A statement of the situation does not necessarily imply that each of the elements is necessarily true; for example, a complaint may be invalid and biased so that all that can be taken for granted is that a complaint has been registered
   2. Considering only one side of a situation – Wherever possible, indicate several alternatives and then point out the reasons you selected the best one
   3. Failing to indicate follow up – Whenever your answer indicates action on your part, make certain that you will take proper follow-up action to see how successful your recommendations, procedures or actions turn out to be
   4. Taking too long in answering any single question – Remember to time your answers properly

EXAMINATION SECTION

RECORD KEEPING
EXAMINATION SECTION
TEST 1

DIRECTIONS: Each question or incomplete statement is followed by several suggested answers or completions. Select the one that BEST answers the question or completes the statement. *PRINT THE LETTER OF THE CORRECT ANSWER IN THE SPACE AT THE RIGHT.*

Questions 1-7.

DIRECTIONS: In answering Questions 1 through 7, use the following master list. For each question, determine where the name would fit on the master list. Each answer choice indicates right before or after the name in the answer choice.

Aaron, Jane
Armstead, Brendan
Bailey, Charles
Dent, Ricardo
Grant, Mark
Mars, Justin
Methieu, Justine
Parker, Cathy
Sampson, Suzy
Thomas, Heather

1. Schmidt, William 1.____
   A. Right before Cathy Parker
   B. Right after Heather Thomas
   C. Right after Suzy Sampson
   D. Right before Ricardo Dent

2. Asanti, Kendall 2.____
   A. Right before Jane Aaron
   B. Right after Charles Bailey
   C. Right before Justine Methieu
   D. Right after Brendan Armstead

3. O'Brien, Daniel 3.____
   A. Right after Justine Methieu
   B. Right before Jane Aaron
   C. Right after Mark Grant
   D. Right before Suzy Sampson

4. Marrow, Alison 4.____
   A. Right before Cathy Parker
   B. Right before Justin Mars
   C. Right before Mark Grant
   D. Right after Heather Thomas

5. Grantt, Marissa 5.____
   A. Right before Mark Grant
   B. Right after Mark Grant
   C. Right after Justin Mars
   D. Right before Suzy Sampson

6. Thompson, Heath 6.____
   A. Right after Justin Mars
   B. Right before Suzy Sampson
   C. Right after Heather Thomas
   D. Right before Cathy Parker

DIRECTIONS: Before answering Question 7, add in all of the names from Questions 1 through 6. Then fit the name in alphabetical order based on the new list.

7. Francisco, Mildred 7.____
   A. Right before Mark Grant
   B. Right after Marissa Grantt
   C. Right before Alison Marrow
   D. Right after Kendall Asanti

Questions 8-10.

DIRECTIONS: In answering Questions 8 through 10, compare each pair of names and addresses. Indicate whether they are the same or different in any way.

8. William H. Pratt, J.D. / Attourney at Law — William H. Pratt, J.D. / Attorney at Law 8.____
   A. No differences
   B. 1 difference
   C. 2 differences
   D. 3 differences

9. 1303 Theater Drive,; Apt. 3-B — 1330 Theatre Drive,; Apt. 3-B 9.____
   A. No differences
   B. 1 difference
   C. 2 differences
   D. 3 differences

10. Petersdorff, Briana and Mary — Petersdorff, Briana and Mary 10.____
   A. No differences
   B. 1 difference
   C. 2 differences
   D. 3 differences

11. Which of the following words, if any, are misspelled? 11.____
   A. Affordable
   B. Circumstansial
   C. Legalese
   D. None of the above

Questions 12-13.

DIRECTIONS: Questions 12 and 13 are to be answered on the basis of the following table.

Standardized Test Results for High School Students in District #1230

	English	Math	Science	Reading
High School 1	21	22	15	18
High School 2	12	16	13	15
High School 3	16	18	21	17
High School 4	19	14	15	16

The scores for each high school in the district were averaged out and listed for each subject tested. Scores of 0-10 are significantly below College Readiness Standards. 11-15 are below College Readiness, 16-20 meet College Readiness, and 21-25 are above College Readiness.

12. If the high schools need to meet or exceed in at least half the categories in order to NOT be considered "at risk," which schools are considered "at risk"? 12.____
    A. High School 2
    B. High School 3
    C. High School 4
    D. Both A and C

13. What percentage of subjects did the district as a whole meet or exceed College Readiness standards? 13.____
    A. 25%
    B. 50%
    C. 75%
    D. 100%

Questions 14-15.

DIRECTIONS: Questions 14 and 15 are to be answered on the basis of the following information.

You have seven employees working as a part of your team: Austin, Emily, Jeremy, Christina, Martin, Harriet, and Steve. You have just sent an e-mail informing them that there will be a mandatory training session next week. To ensure that work still gets done, you are offering the training twice during the week: once on Tuesday and also on Thursday. This way half the employees will still be working while the other half attend the training. The only other issue is that Jeremy doesn't work on Tuesdays and Harriet doesn't work on Thursdays due to compressed work schedules.

14. Which of the following is a possible attendance roster for the first training session? 14.____
    A. Emily, Jeremy, Steve
    B. Steve, Christina, Harriet
    C. Harriet, Jeremy, Austin
    D. Steve, Martin, Jeremy

15. If Harriet, Christina, and Steve attend the training session on Tuesday, which of the following is a possible roster for Thursday's training session? 15.____
    A. Jeremy, Emily, and Austin
    B. Emily, Martin, and Harriet
    C. Austin, Christina, and Emily
    D. Jeremy, Emily, and Steve

Questions 16-20.

DIRECTIONS: In answering Questions 16 through 20, you will be given a word and will need to choose the answer choice that is MOST similar or different to the word.

16. Which word means the SAME as *annual*? 16.____
    A. Monthly
    B. Usually
    C. Yearly
    D. Constantly

17. Which word means the SAME as *effort*? 17.____
    A. Energy
    B. Equate
    C. Cherish
    D. Commence

18. Which word means the OPPOSITE of *forlorn*? 18.____
    A. Neglected
    B. Lethargy
    C. Optimistic
    D. Astonished

19. Which word means the SAME as *risk*? 19.____
    A. Admire
    B. Hazard
    C. Limit
    D. Hesitant

20. Which word means the OPPOSITE of *translucent*? 20.____
A. Opaque B. Transparent C. Luminous D. Introverted

21. Last year, Jamie's annual salary was $50,000. Her boss called her today to inform her that she would receive a 20% raise for the upcoming year. How much more money will Jamie receive next year? 21.____
A. $60,000 B. $10,000 C. $1,000 D. $51,000

22. You and a co-worker work for a temp hiring agency as part of their office staff. You both are given 6 days off per month. How many days off are you and your co-worker given in a year? 22.____
A. 24 B. 72 C. 144 D. 48

23. If Margot makes $34,000 per year and she works 40 hours per week for all 52 weeks, what is her hourly rate? 23.____
A. $16.34/hour B. $17.00/hour C. $15.54/hour D. $13.23/hour

24. How many dimes are there in $175.00? 24.____
A. 175 B. 1,750 C. 3,500 D. 17,500

25. If Janey is three times as old as Emily, and Emily is 3, how old is Janey? 25.____
A. 6 B. 9 C. 12 D. 15

KEY (CORRECT ANSWERS)

1. C
2. D
3. A
4. B
5. B

6. C
7. A
8. B
9. C
10. A

11. B
12. A
13. D
14. B
15. A

16. C
17. A
18. C
19. B
20. A

21. B
22. C
23. A
24. B
25. B

TEST 2

DIRECTIONS: Each question or incomplete statement is followed by several suggested answers or completions. Select the one that BEST answers the question or completes the statement. *PRINT THE LETTER OF THE CORRECT ANSWER IN THE SPACE AT THE RIGHT.*

Questions 1-6.

DIRECTIONS: Questions 1 through 6 are to be answered on the basis of the following information.

item	name of item to be ordered
quantity	minimum number that can be ordered
beginning amount	amount in stock at start of month
amount received	amount receiving during month
ending amount	amount in stock at end of month
amount used	amount used during month
amount to order	will need at least as much of each item as used in the previous month
unit price	cost of each unit of an item
total price	total price for the order

Item	Quantity	Beginning	Received	Ending	Amount Used	Amount to Order	Unit Price	Total Price
Pens	10	22	10	8	24	20	$0.11	$2.20
Spiral notebooks	8	30	13	12			$0.25	
Binder clips	2 boxes	3 boxes	1 box	1 box			$1.79	
Sticky notes	3 packs	12 packs	4 packs	2 packs			$1.29	
Dry erase markers	1 pack (dozen)	34 markers	8 markers	40 markers			$16.49	
Ink cartridges (printer)	1 cartridge	3 cartridges	1 cartridge	2 cartridges			$79.99	
Folders	10 folders	25 folders	15 folders	10 folders			$1.08	

1. How many packs of sticky notes were used during the month? 1.____
   A. 16 B. 10 C. 12 D. 14

2. How many folders need to be ordered for next month? 2.____
   A. 15 B. 20 C. 30 D. 40

3. What is the total price of notebooks that you will need to order? 3.____
   A. $6.00 B. $0.25 C. $4.50 D. $2.75

4. Which of the following will you spend the second most money on? 4.____
   A. Ink cartridges B. Dry erase markers
   C. Sticky notes D. Binder clips

5. How many packs of dry erase markers should you order? 5.____
   A. 1 B. 8 C. 12 D. 0

6. What will be the total price of the file folders you order? 6.____
A. $20.16 B. $21.60 C. $10.80 D. $4.32

Questions 7-11.

DIRECTIONS: Questions 7 through 11 are to be answered on the basis of the following table.

Number of Car Accidents, By Location and Cause, for 2014						
	Location 1		Location 2		Location 3	
Cause	Number	Percent	Number	Percent	Number	Percent
Severe Weather	10		25		30	
Excessive Speeding	20	40	5		10	
Impaired Driving	15		15	25	8	
Miscellaneous	5		15		2	4
TOTALS	50	100	60	100	50	100

7. Which of the following is the third highest cause of accidents for all three locations? 7.____
A. Severe Weather
B. Impaired Driving
C. Miscellaneous
D. Excessive Speeding

8. The average number of Severe Weather accidents per week at Location 3 for the year (52 weeks) was MOST NEARLY 8.____
A. 0.57 B. 30 C. 1 D. 1.25

9. Which location had the LARGEST percentage of accidents caused by Impaired Driving? 9.____
A. 1 B. 2 C. 3 D. Both A and B

10. If one-third of the accidents at all three locations resulted in at least one fatality, what is the LEAST amount of deaths caused by accidents last year? 10.____
A. 60 B. 106 C. 66 D. 53

11. What is the percentage of accidents caused by miscellaneous means from all three locations in 2014? 11.____
A. 5% B. 10% C. 13% D. 25%

12. How many pairs of the following groups of letters are exactly alike? 12.____

ACDOBJ	ACDBOJ
HEWBWR	HEWRWB
DEERVS	DEERVS
BRFQSX	BRFQSX
WEYRVB	WEYRVB
SPQRZA	SQRPZA

A. 2 B. 3 C. 4 D. 5

Questions 13-19.

DIRECTIONS: Questions 13 through 19 are to be answered on the basis of the following information.

In 2012, the most current information on the American population was finished. The information was compiled by 200 volunteers in each of the 50 states. The territory of Puerto Rico, a sovereign of the United States, had 25 people assigned to compile data. In February of 2010, volunteers in each state and sovereign began collecting information. In Puerto Rico, data collection finished by January 31st, 2011, while work in the United States was completed on June 30, 2012. Each volunteer gathered data on the population of their state or sovereign. When the information was compiled, volunteers sent reports to the nation's capital, Washington, D.C. Each volunteer worked 20 hours per month and put together 10 reports per month. After the data was compiled in total, 50 people reviewed the data and worked from January 2012 to December 2012.

13. How many reports were generated from February 2010 to April 2010 in Illinois and Ohio? 13.____
A. 3,000 B. 6,000 C. 12,000 D. 15,000

14. How many volunteers in total collected population data in January 2012? 14.____
A. 10,000 B. 2,000 C. 225 D. 200

15. How many reports were put together in May 2012? 15.____
A. 2,000 B. 50,000 C. 100,000 D. 100,250

16. How many hours did the Puerto Rican volunteers work in the fall (September-November)? 16.____
A. 60 B. 500 C. 1,500 D. 0

17. How many workers were compiling or reviewing data in July 2012? 17.____
A. 25 B. 50 C. 200 D. 250

18. What was the total amount of hours worked by Nevada volunteers in July 2010? 18.____
A. 500 B. 4,000 C. 4,500 D. 5,000

19. How many reviewers worked in January 2013? 19.____
A. 75 B. 50 C. 0 D. 25

20. John has to file 10 documents per shelf. How many documents would it take for John to fill 40 shelves? 20.____
A. 40 B. 400 C. 4,500 D. 5,000

21. Jill wants to travel from New York City to Los Angeles by bike, which is approximately 2,772 miles. How many miles per day would Jill need to average if she wanted to complete the trip in 4 weeks? 21.____
A. 100 B. 89 C. 99 D. 94

22. If there are 24 CPU's and only 7 monitors, how many more monitors do you need to have the same amount of monitors as CPU's? 22.____
    A. Not enough information
    B. 17
    C. 31
    D. 0

23. If Gerry works 5 days a week and 8 hours each day, and John works 3 days a week and 10 hours each day, how many more hours per year will Gerry work than John? 23.____
    A. They work the same amount of hours.
    B. 450
    C. 520
    D. 832

24. Jimmy gets transferred to a new office. The new office has 25 employees, but only 16 are there due to a blizzard. How many coworkers was Jimmy able to meet on his first day? 24.____
    A. 16
    B. 25
    C. 9
    D. 7

25. If you do a fundraiser for charities in your area and raise $500 total, how much would you give to each charity if you were donating equal amounts to 3 of them? 25.____
    A. $250.00
    B. $167.77
    C. $50.00
    D. $111.11

KEY (CORRECT ANSWERS)

1.	D	11.	C
2.	B	12.	B
3.	A	13.	C
4.	C	14.	A
5.	D	15.	C
6.	B	16.	C
7.	D	17.	B
8.	A	18.	B
9.	A	19.	C
10.	D	20.	B

21.	C
22.	B
23.	C
24.	A
25.	B

TEST 3

DIRECTIONS: Each question or incomplete statement is followed by several suggested answers or completions. Select the one that BEST answers the question or completes the statement. *PRINT THE LETTER OF THE CORRECT ANSWER IN THE SPACE AT THE RIGHT.*

Questions 1-3.

DIRECTIONS: In answering Questions 1 through 3, choose the correctly spelled word.

1. A. allusion B. alusion C. allusien D. allution 1.____

2. A. altitude B. alltitude C. atlitude D. altlitude 2.____

3. A. althogh B. allthough C. althrough D. although 3.____

Questions 4-9.

DIRECTIONS: In answering Questions 4 through 9, choose the answer that BEST completes the analogy.

4. Odometer is to mileage as compass is to 4.____
   A. speed B. needle C. hiking D. direction

5. Marathon is to race as hibernation is to 5.____
   A. winter B. dream C. sleep D. bear

6. Cup is to coffee as bowl is to 6.____
   A. dish B. spoon C. food D. soup

7. Flow is to river as stagnant is to 7.____
   A. pool B. rain C. stream D. canal

8. Paw is to cat as hoof is to 8.____
   A. lamb B. horse C. lion D. elephant

9. Architect is to building as sculptor is to 9.____
   A. museum B. chisel C. stone D. statue

Questions 10-14.

DIRECTIONS: Questions 10 through 14 are to be answered on the basis of the following graph.

Population of Carroll City Broken Down by Age and Gender (in Thousands)			
Age	Female	Male	Total
Under 15	60	60	120
15-23		22	
24-33		20	44
34-43	13	18	31
44-53	20		67
64 and Over	65	65	130
TOTAL	230	232	462

10. How many people in the city are between the ages of 15-23? 10.____
    A. 70 B. 46,000 C. 70,000 D. 225,000

11. Approximately what percentage of the total population of the city was female aged 24-33? 11.____
    A. 10% B. 5% C. 15% D. 25%

12. If 33% of the males have a job and 55% of females don't have a job, which of the following statements is TRUE? 12.____
    A. Males have approximately 2,600 more jobs than females.
    B. Females have approximately 49,000 more jobs than males.
    C. Females have approximately 26,000 more jobs than males.
    D. None of the above statements are true.

13. How many females between the ages of 15-23 live in Carroll City? 13.____
    A. 67,000 B. 24,000 C. 48,000 D. 91,000

14. Assume all males 44-53 living in Carroll City are employed. If two-thirds of males age 44-53 work jobs outside of Carroll City, how many work within city limits? 14.____
    A. 31,333
    B. 15,667
    C. 47,000
    D. Cannot answer the question with the information provided

Questions 15-16.

DIRECTIONS: Questions 15 and 16 are labeled as shown. Alphabetize them for filing. Choose the answer that correctly shows the order.

15. (1) AED
(2) OOS
(3) FOA
(4) DOM
(5) COB

15.____

A. 2-5-4-3-2   B. 1-4-5-2-3   C. 1-5-4-2-3   D. 1-5-4-3-2

16. Alphabetize the names of the people. Last names are given last.
(1) Lindsey Jamestown
(2) Jane Alberta
(3) Ally Jamestown
(4) Allison Johnston
(5) Lyle Moreno

16.____

A. 2-1-3-4-5   B. 3-4-2-1-5   C. 2-3-1-4-5   D. 4-3-2-1-5

17. Which of the following words is misspelled?

17.____

A. disgust   B. whisper
C. locale   D. none of the above

Questions 18-21.

DIRECTIONS: Questions 18 through 21 are to be answered on the basis of the following list of employees.

Robertson, Aaron
Bacon, Gina
Jerimiah, Trace
Gillette, Stanley
Jacks, Sharon

18. Which employee name would come in third in alphabetized list?

18.____

A. Robertson, Aaron   B. Jerimiah, Trace
C. Gillette, Stanley   D. Jacks, Sharon

19. Which employee's first name starts with the letter in the alphabet that is five letters after the first letter of their last name?

19.____

A. Jerimiah, Trace   B. Bacon, Gina
C. Jacks, Sharon   D. Gillette, Stanley

20. How many employees have last names that are exactly five letters long?

20.____

A. 1   B. 2   C. 3   D. 4

21. How many of the employees have either a first or last name that starts with the letter "G"? 21.____
A. 1 B. 2 C. 4 D. 5

Questions 22-25.

DIRECTIONS: Questions 22 through 25 are to be answered on the basis of the following chart.

Bicycle Sales (Model #34JA32)							
Country	May	June	July	August	September	October	Total
Germany	34	47	45	54	56	60	296
Britain	40	44	36	47	47	46	260
Ireland	37	32	32	32	34	33	200
Portugal	14	14	14	16	17	14	89
Italy	29	29	28	31	29	31	177
Belgium	22	24	24	26	25	23	144
Total	176	198	179	206	208	207	1166

22. What percentage of the overall total was sold to the German importer? 22.____
A. 25.3% B. 22% C. 24.1% D. 23%

23. What percentage of the overall total was sold in September? 23.____
A. 24.1% B. 25.6% C. 17.9% D. 24.6%

24. What is the average number of units per month imported into Belgium over the first four months shown? 24.____
A. 26 B. 20 C. 24 D. 31

25. If you look at the three smallest importers, what is their total import percentage? 25.____
A. 35.1% B. 37.1% C. 40% D. 28%

KEY (CORRECT ANSWERS)

1. A
2. A
3. D
4. D
5. C

6. D
7. A
8. B
9. D
10. C

11. B
12. C
13. C
14. B
15. D

16. C
17. D
18. D
19. B
20. B

21. B
22. A
23. C
24. C
25. A

TEST 4

DIRECTIONS: Each question or incomplete statement is followed by several suggested answers or completions. Select the one that BEST answers the question or completes the statement. *PRINT THE LETTER OF THE CORRECT ANSWER IN THE SPACE AT THE RIGHT.*

Questions 1-6.

DIRECTIONS: In answering Questions 1 through 6, choose the sentence that represents the BEST example of English grammar.

1. A. Joey and me want to go on a vacation next week. 1.____
   B. Gary told Jim he would need to take some time off.
   C. If turning six years old, Jim's uncle would teach Spanish to him.
   D. Fax a copy of your resume to Ms. Perez and me.

2. A. Jerry stood in line for almost two hours. 2.____
   B. The reaction to my engagement was less exciting than I thought it would be.
   C. Carlos and me have done great work on this project.
   D. Two parts of the speech needs to be revised before tomorrow.

3. A. Arriving home, the alarm was tripped. 3.____
   B. Jonny is regarded as a stand up guy, a responsible parent, and he doesn't give up until a task is finished.
   C. Each employee must submit a drug test each month.
   D. One of the documents was incinerated in the explosion.

4. A. As soon as my parents get home, I told them I finished all of my chores. 4.____
   B. I asked my teacher to send me my missing work, check my absences, and how did I do on my test.
   C. Matt attempted to keep it concealed from Jenny and me.
   D. If Mary or him cannot get work done on time, I will have to split them up.

5. A. Driving to work, the traffic report warned him of an accident on Highway 47. 5.____
   B. Jimmy has performed well this season.
   C. Since finishing her degree, several job offers have been given to Cam.
   D. Our boss is creating unstable conditions for we employees.

6. A. The thief was described as a tall man with a wiry mustache weighing approximately 150 pounds. 6.____
   B. She gave Patrick and I some more time to finish our work.
   C. One of the books that he ordered was damaged in shipping.
   D. While talking on the rotary phone, the car Jim was driving skidded off the road.

Questions 7-9.

DIRECTIONS: Questions 7 through 9 are to be answered on the basis of the following graph.

Ice Lake Frozen Flight (2002-2013)		
Year	Number of Participants	Temperature (Fahrenheit)
2002	22	4°
2003	50	33°
2004	69	18°
2005	104	22°
2006	108	24°
2007	288	33°
2008	173	9°
2009	598	39°
2010	698	26°
2011	696	30°
2012	777	28°
2013	578	32°

7. Which two year span had the LARGEST difference between temperatures? 7.____
   A. 2002 and 2003
   B. 2011 and 2012
   C. 2008 and 2009
   D. 2003 and 2004

8. How many total people participated in the years after the temperature reached at least 29°? 8.____
   A. 2,295
   B. 1,717
   C. 2,210
   D. 4,543

9. In 2007, the event saw 288 participants, while in 2008 that number dropped to 173. Which of the following reasons BEST explains the drop in participants? 9.____
   A. The event had not been going on that long and people didn't know about it.
   B. The lake water wasn't cold enough to have people jump in.
   C. The temperature was too cold for many people who would have normally participated.
   D. None of the above reasons explain the drop in participants.

10. In the following list of numbers, how many times does 4 come just after 2 when 2 comes just after an odd number? 10.____
    2365247653898632488572486392424
    A. 2
    B. 3
    C. 4
    D. 5

11. Which choice below lists the letter that is as far after B as S is after N in the alphabet? 11.____
    A. G
    B. H
    C. I
    D. J

Questions 12-15.

DIRECTIONS: Questions 12 through 15 are to be answered on the basis of the following directory and list of changes.

Directory		
Name	Emp. Type	Position
Julie Taylor	Warehouse	Packer
James King	Office	Administrative Assistant
John Williams	Office	Salesperson
Ray Moore	Warehouse	Maintenance
Kathleen Byrne	Warehouse	Supervisor
Amy Jones	Office	Salesperson
Paul Jonas	Office	Salesperson
Lisa Wong	Warehouse	Loader
Eugene Lee	Office	Accountant
Bruce Lavine	Office	Manager
Adam Gates	Warehouse	Packer
Will Suter	Warehouse	Packer
Gary Lorper	Office	Accountant
Jon Adams	Office	Salesperson
Susannah Harper	Office	Salesperson

Directory Updates:

- Employee e-mail addresses will adhere to the following guidelines: lastnamefirstname@apexindustries.com (ex. Susannah Harper is harpersusannah@apexindustries.com). Currently, employees in the warehouse share one e-mail, distribution@apexindustries.com.
- The "Loader" position will now be referred to as "Specialist I"
- Adam Gates has accepted a Supervisor position within the Warehouse and is no longer a Packer. All warehouse employees report to the two Supervisors and all office employees report to the Manager.

12. Amy Jones tried to send an e-mail to Adam Gates, but it wouldn't send. Which of the following offers the BEST explanation? 12.____
    A. Amy put Adam's first name first and then his last name.
    B. Adam doesn't check his e-mail, so he wouldn't know if he received the e-mail or not.
    C. Adam does not have his own e-mail.
    D. Office employees are not allowed to send e-mails to each other.

13. How many Packers currently work for Apex Industries? 13.____
    A. 2 B. 3 C. 4 D. 5

14. What position does Lisa Wong currently hold? 14.____
    A. Specialist I
    B. Secretary
    C. Administrative Assistant
    D. Loader

15. If an employee wanted to contact the office manager, which of the following e-mails should the e-mail be sent to? 15.____
    A. officemanager@apexindustries.com
    B. brucelavine@apexindustries.com
    C. lavinebruce@apexindustries.com
    D. distribution@apexindustries.com

Questions 16-19.

DIRECTIONS: In answering Questions 16 through 19, compare the three names, numbers or addresses.

16. Smiley Yarnell   Smiley Yarnel   Smily Yarnell 16.____
    A. All three are exactly alike.
    B. The first and second are exactly alike.
    C. The second and third are exactly alike.
    D. All three are different.

17. 1583 Theater Drive   1583 Theater Drive   1583 Theatre Drive 17.____
    A. All three are exactly alike.
    B. The first and second are exactly alike.
    C. The second and third are exactly alike.
    D. All three are different.

18. 3341893212   3341893212   3341893212 18.____
    A. All three are exactly alike.
    B. The first and second are exactly alike.
    C. The second and third are exactly alike.
    D. All three are different.

19. Douglass Watkins   Douglas Watkins   Douglass Watkins 19.____
    A. All three are exactly alike.
    B. The first and third are exactly alike.
    C. The second and third are exactly alike.
    D. All three are different.

Questions 20-24.

DIRECTIONS: In answering Questions 20 through 24, you will be presented with a word. Choose the synonym that BEST represents the word in question.

20. Flexible 20.____
    A. delicate   B. inflammable   C. strong   D. pliable

21. Alternative 21.____
    A. choice   B. moderate   C. lazy   D. value

22. Corroborate 22.____
   A. examine B. explain C. verify D. explain

23. Respiration 23.____
   A. recovery B. breathing C. sweating D. selfish

24. Negligent 24.____
   A. lazy B. moderate C. hopeless D. lax

25. Plumber is to Wrench as Painter is to 25.____
   A. pipe B. shop C. hammer D. brush

KEY (CORRECT ANSWERS)

1.	D	11.	A
2.	A	12.	C
3.	D	13.	A
4.	C	14.	A
5.	B	15.	C
6.	C	16.	D
7.	C	17.	B
8.	B	18.	A
9.	C	19.	B
10.	C	20.	D

21.	A
22.	C
23.	B
24.	D
25.	D

EXAMINATION SECTION
TEST 1

DIRECTIONS: Each question or incomplete statement is followed by several suggested answers or completions. Select the one that BEST answers the question or completes the statement. *PRINT THE LETTER OF THE CORRECT ANSWER IN THE SPACE AT THE RIGHT.*

Questions 1-7.

DIRECTIONS: Questions 1 through 7 are to be answered on the basis of the following income statement.

Laura Lee's Bridal Shop
Income Statement
For the Year Ended December 31, 2018

Revenue:		
New & Used Bridal Gowns & Accessories		$55,000
Expenses:		
Advertisement Expense	$ 2,000	
Salaries Expense	12,000	
Dry cleaning & Alterations	10,000	
Utilities	1,500	
Total Expenses		25,500
Net Income		$29,500

1. What is the period of time covered by this income statement? 1.____

   A. January-December 2017
   B. December 2018
   C. January 2017-December 2018
   D. January-December 2018

2. What is the source of the revenue? 2.____

   A. New and used bridal gowns, advertisements, salaries, dry cleaning, and utilities
   B. Advertisements, salaries, dry cleaning, alterations, and utilities
   C. New and used bridal gowns and accessories
   D. Net income

3. What is the total revenue? 3.____

   A. $25,500 B. $55,000 C. $29,500 D. $79,500

4. Which of the following are expenses? 4.____

   A. Salaries
   B. New and used bridal gowns and accessories
   C. Revenue
   D. New and used bridal gowns, advertisements, and dry cleaning

5. What are the total expenses? 5.____

   A. $55,000 B. $29,500 C. $79,500 D. $25,500

6. There is a resulting net income because 6.____

   A. total revenue and total expenses are combined
   B. net income is greater than total revenue
   C. the total revenue is greater than total expenses
   D. the total revenue is less than total expenses

7. Is this statement an interim statement? 7.____

   A. *Yes*, because it covers an entire accounting period
   B. *No*, because it covers an entire accounting period
   C. *Yes*, because it covers a period of less than a year
   D. *No*, because it covers a period of more than a year

8. What is the name of the accounting report that may show either a net profit or a net loss for an accounting period? 8.____

   A. Income statement
   B. Balance sheet
   C. Statement of capital
   D. Classified balance sheet

9. What are the two main parts of the body of the income statement? 9.____

   A. Cash and Capital
   B. Revenue and Expenses
   C. Liabilities and Capital
   D. Assets and Notes Payable

10. If total revenue exceeds total expenses for an accounting period, what is the difference called? 10.____

    A. Gross income
    B. Total liabilities
    C. Total assets
    D. Net income

11. In the body of a balance sheet, what are the three sections called? 11.____

    A. Assets and liabilities
    B. Cash, liabilities, and revenue
    C. Assets, liabilities, and capital
    D. Revenue, assets, and capital

12. What business record shows the results of the proprietor's borrowing assets from the business, usually in anticipation of profits? 12.____

    A. Proprietor's withdrawals
    B. Accounts payable
    C. Liabilities and Capital
    D. Total liabilities

Questions 13-24.

DIRECTIONS: For each transaction given for Mona's Magic Moments Hair Salon in Questions 13 through 24, identify which journal the transaction should be recorded in.

13. April 1: Mona, the owner, paid the month's rent - $600.00; check no. 356. 13.____

    A. General
    B. Cash disbursements
    C. Purchases
    D. Sales

14. April 6: the salon purchased $300.00 worth of styling products on account from Pomme de Terre Company. 14.____

A. Cash disbursements
B. General
C. Sales
D. Purchases

15. April 8: sold $100.00 worth of hair products on account to Mrs. Angela Bray. 15.____

A. Sales
B. Purchases
C. Cash disbursements
D. General

16. April 11: the owner, Mona Ramen, withdrew $80.00 of styling products for personal use. 16.____

A. Sales
B. Cash receipts
C. General
D. Cash disbursements

17. April 13: paid Pomme de Terre Company $300.00 on account; check 357. 17.____

A. Purchases
B. Cash disbursements
C. Cash receipts
D. General

18. April 15: cash sales to date were $4,607.00. 18.____

A. Cash disbursements
B. Purchases
C. Sales
D. General

19. April 17: issued credit slip #17 to Mrs. Angela Bray for $25.00 for merchandise returned. 19.____

A. Cash disbursements
B. Cash receipts
C. Sales
D. General

20. April 19: paid electric bill for $250.00; check no. 358. 20.____

A. Cash disbursements
B. Purchases
C. General
D. Cash receipts

21. April 21: received $75.00 from Mrs. Angela Bray for balance due on account. 21.____

A. Sales
B. Cash disbursements
C. Cash receipts
D. Purchases

22. April 23: sold $88.00 of hair products on account to Ms. Tania Alioto. 22.____

A. Purchases
B. Sales
C. Cash disbursements
D. Cash receipts

23. April 27: purchased $500.00 of equipment from Salon Stylings Merchandisers on account. 23.____

A. Cash disbursements
B. Sales
C. General
D. Purchases

24. April 30: cash sales to date were $5023.00. 24.____

A. Purchases
B. Sales
C. Cash receipts
D. General

Questions 25-30.

DIRECTIONS: Questions 25 through 30 are to be answered on the basis of the following ledger for a barbecue take-out restaurant owned and operated by Ruby Joiner.

Cash	
450	150
212	125
328	440
172	125
250	70
275	150
325	50

Accounts Receivable	
360	170
250	100
165	120
100	60

Delivery Equipment	
5,000	
4,000	
3,000	

Supplies	
40	
65	
30	
25	

Ruby Joiner, Capital	
	8,200
	2,000
	2,097

Accounts Payable	
10	600
15	300
	200

Ruby Joiner, Drawing	
225	
175	
200	

Advertising Expense	
40	
45	

Delivery Income	
	400
	350
	250
	100

Trucking Expense	
100	
50	

Telephone Expense	
80	
40	
20	

25. What is the balance on the Cash account shown above? 25.____

A. 2,012.00 B. 1,110.00 C. 3,122.00 D. 902.00

26. What is the balance on the Accounts receivable account shown above? 26.____

A. 425.00 B. 875.00 C. 450.00 D. 1315.00

27. What is the balance on the Accounts payable account shown above? 27.____

A. 1100.00 B. 1075.00 C. 25.00 D. 1125.00

28. Which of the above accounts has a balance of 1100.00? 28.____

A. Accounts payable
B. Delivery Income
C. Cash
D. Delivery equipment

29. Which of the above accounts has a balance of 12,000.00? 29.____

A. Ruby Joiner, Capital
B. Cash and Accounts receivable combined
C. Delivery equipment
D. None of the accounts

30. If you made a balance sheet out of the information listed above, Ruby Joiner's total assets would be 30.____

A. 14,472.00 B. 12,297.00 C. 13,392.00 D. 13,487.00

Questions 31-34.

DIRECTIONS: Questions 31 through 34 are to be answered on the basis of the following information, to be included on a checking deposit ticket.

Five $20 bills; 11 $10 bills; 6 $5 bills; 47 $1 bills; 200 half dollars; 120 quarters; 112 dimes; 320 nickels; 67 pennies. Second National Bank (73-124) check of 152.34; Bank of the Midwest (13-298) check of 68.37; Great National Bank (32-165) check of 185.06.

31. What is the TOTAL currency for this deposit? 31.____

A. $387 B. $287 C. $444.87 D. $157.87

32. What is the TOTAL coin for this deposit? 32.____

A. $387 B. $287 C. $444.87 D. $157.87

33. What is the check total for this deposit? 33.____

A. $692.77 B. $406 C. $405.77 D. $850.64

34. What is the TOTAL deposit? 34.____

A. $444.87 B. $692.77 C. $851 D. $850.64

Questions 35-37.

DIRECTIONS: Questions 35 through 37 are to be answered on the basis of the following petty cash journal.

Date	Receipt No.	To Whom Paid	For What	Acct.#	Amount
10/2	1	Anna Jones - Mail	Postage	548	13.50
10/2	2	Jim Collins	Messenger	525	5.75
10/4	3	Anna Jones - Mail	Postage	548	13.50
10/5	4	Lucky Stores	Coffee	515	7.34
10/6	5	Tom Allen	Lunch w/customer	525	11.38

35. What is the TOTAL disbursement from this fund for the time period 10/1 through 10/6? 35.____

A. $51.47 B. $40.09 C. $61.47 D. $26.59

36. How much money was disbursed to Account #548 during the time period 10/1-10/16? 36.____

A. $51.47 B. $26 C. $27 D. $34.34

37. If the fund began the month with a total of $100.00, what amount was left in the fund at the end of business on 10/5? 37.____

A. $48.53 B. $59.91 C. $51.47 D. $40.09

Questions 38-40.

DIRECTIONS: Questions 38 through 40 are to be answered on the basis of the following information.

A promissory note dated December 1, 2018, bearing interest at a rate of 12% and due in 90 days, is sent to a creditor. The face value of the note is $900.

38. What is the due date of the promissory note? 38.____

A. January 15, 2019
B. March 1, 2019
C. February 1, 2019
D. December 31, 2018

39. What is the TOTAL interest that will be earned on the note? 39.____

A. $27
B. $270
C. $108
D. $10.80

40. What interest will be earned on the note for the old accounting period (December 1-31)? 40.____

A. $90
B. $36
C. $9
D. $3.60

KEY (CORRECT ANSWERS)

1. D	11. C	21. C	31. B
2. C	12. A	22. B	32. D
3. B	13. B	23. D	33. C
4. A	14. D	24. B	34. D
5. D	15. A	25. D	35. A
6. C	16. C	26. A	36. C
7. B	17. B	27. B	37. B
8. A	18. C	28. B	38. B
9. B	19. D	29. C	39. A
10. D	20. A	30. D	40. C

TEST 2

DIRECTIONS: Each question or incomplete statement is followed by several suggested answers or completions. Select the one that BEST answers the question or completes the statement. *PRINT THE LETTER OF THE CORRECT ANSWER IN THE SPACE AT THE RIGHT.*

Questions 1-4.

DIRECTIONS: Questions 1 through 4 are to be answered on the basis of the following information, to be included in a deposit slip.

14 twenty dollar bills	63 quarters
52 ten dollar bills	22 dimes
12 five dollar bills	44 nickels
43 one dollar bills	70 pennies

Checks: $236.34 and $129.72

1. What is the TOTAL amount of currency for this deposit? 1.____

   A. $923.85 B. $1269.06 C. $903.00 D. $1299.91

2. What is the TOTAL amount of coin for this deposit? 2.____

   A. $20.85 B. $923.85 C. $903.00 D. $1299.91

3. What is the TOTAL amount of check for this deposit? 3.____

   A. $20.85 B. $366.06 C. $1299.91 D. $903.00

4. What is the TOTAL deposit for this slip? 4.____

   A. $1269.06 B. $903.00 C. $923.85 D. $1289.91

Questions 5-7.

DIRECTIONS: Questions 5 through 7 are to be answered on the basis of the following information.

Angela Martinez's last check stub balance was $675.50. Her bank statement balance dated April 30 was $652.00. A $250 deposit was in transit on that date. Outstanding checks were as follows: No. 127, $65.00; No. 129, $203.50; No. 130, $50.00. The bank service charge for the month was $5.00.

5. What was Angela Martinez's available checkbook balance on April 30? 5.____

   A. $652.00 B. $338.50 C. $583.50 D. $675.50

6. In order to reconcile her checkbook balance with her bank statement balance, what must Angela Martinez do? 6.____

   A. Add her checkbook balance to the balance on her bank statement
   B. Subtract her checkbook balance from the balance on her bank statement

C. Ignore her checkbook balance and adopt the balance on her bank statement
D. Adjust the checkbook balance by adding deposits and debiting outstanding checks and charges

7. The check stub balance referred to in the problem refers to the 7.____

A. last check Angela Martinez recorded in her checkbook
B. amount of money left in Angela Martinez's account according to her own calculations based on the checks, charges, and deposits she has written and recorded
C. amount of money left in Angela Martinez's account according to the bank's calculations based on the checks, charges, and deposits posted to her account
D. number of checks left in her checkbook

Questions 8-9.

DIRECTIONS: Questions 8 and 9 are to be answered on the basis of the following information.

Tu Nguyen, an interior designer, received his June bank statement on July 2. The balance was $622.66. His last check stub balance was $700. On comparing the two, he noticed that a deposit of $275 made on June 30 was not included on the statement; also, a bank service charge of $4 was deducted. Outstanding checks were as follows: No. 331, $97.50; No. 332, $207; No. 335, $25.40; and No. 336, $68.97.

8. What is Nguyen's CORRECT available bank balance? 8.____

A. $494.79 B. $897.66 C. $700.00 D. $219.79

9. The bank statement balance referred to in the problem refers to the 9.____

A. last check Tu Nguyen recorded in his checkbook
B. last check presented for payment to Tu Nguyen's account
C. amount of money left in Tu Nguyen's account according to the bank's calculations based on the checks, charges, and deposits posted to his account
D. amount of money left in Tu Nguyen's account based on his own calculations of the checks, charges, and deposits he has written and recorded

10. What of the following endorsements would be an example of a simple Endorsement in Blank? 10.____

A. Pay to the Order of Joanie Anderson
B. Joanie Anderson
C. For deposit only; Acct. No. 12345; Joanie Anderson
D. Without Recourse; Joanie Anderson

11. Which of the following endorsements would limit the further purpose or use of the endorsed check? 11.____

A. Pay to the Order of Joanie Anderson
B. Joanie Anderson
C. For deposit only; Acct. No. 12345; Joanie Anderson,
D. Without Recourse; Joanie Anderson

12. Which of the following endorsements would protect the endorser from legal responsibility for payment, should the drawer have insufficient funds to honor his/her own check? 12.____

    A. Pay to the Order of Joanie Anderson
    B. Joanie Anderson
    C. For deposit only; Acct. No. 12345; Joanie Anderson
    D. Without Recourse; Joanie Anderson

Questions 13-24.

DIRECTIONS: Questions 13 - 24 are to be answered on the basis of the following ledger accounts for Wheelsmith Organic Farms.

Wheelsmith Organic Farms
Ledger Accounts

Cash		Accounts Payable		Service Supplies	
Jan. 1 4,000			Jan. 1 2,000	Jan. 1 2,000	

Shelley Wheelsmith, Capital		Machinery	
	Jan. 1 11,000	Jan. 1 7,000	

13. Transaction #1: On January 5, Shelley Wheelsmith, the proprietor, received cash amounting to $5,000 as a result of returning machinery that had recently been purchased. What account(s) should this transaction be posted to? 13.____

    A. Cash
    B. Cash and Machinery
    C. Machinery
    D. Cash, Machinery, and Service Supplies

14. Transaction #2: On January 8, Shelley Wheelsmith, the proprietor, sent out a check for $600 in partial payment of the accounts payable. What account(s) should this transaction be posted to? 14.____

    A. Accounts Payable
    B. Accounts Payable and Cash
    C. Accounts Payable and Capital
    D. Cash

15. Transaction #3: On January 14, Shelley Wheelsmith, proprietor, made an additional investment in the business by contributing machinery valued at $1,500. What account(s) should this transaction be posted to? 15.____

    A. Machinery
    B. Machinery and Capital
    C. Capital
    D. Machinery and Cash

16. Transaction #4: On January 26, Shelley Wheelsmith, proprietor, purchased additional service supplies for $200. She agreed to pay the obligation in 30 days. What account(s) should this transaction be posted to? 16.____

A. Accounts Payable and Liabilities
B. Service supplies
C. Accounts Payable
D. Accounts Payable and Service supplies

17. Transaction #5: On January 31, Shelley Wheelsmith, proprietor, purchased service supplies paying cash of $50. What account(s) should this transaction be posted to? 17.____

A. Service supplies
B. Service supplies and Accounts Payable
C. Cash and Service supplies
D. Cash

18. What is the balance in the Cash account after all of these transactions are posted? 18.____

A. $9,000 B. $1,000 C. $5,000 D. $8,350

19. What is the balance in the Machinery account after all of these transactions are posted? 19.____

A. $7,000 B. $5,000 C. $3,500 D. $13,500

20. What is the balance in the Accounts Payable account after all of these transactions are posted? 20.____

A. $800 B. $600 C. $2,600 D. $1,600

21. What is the balance in the Capital account after all of these transactions are posted? 21.____

A. $12,500 B. $800 C. $11,600 D. $10,400

22. What is the balance in the Service supplies account after all of these transactions are posted? 22.____

A. $2,000 B. $2,250 C. $750 D. $2,200

23. What are the total assets of Wheelsmith Organic Farms after these transactions have been posted? 23.____

A. $10,600 B. $11,850 C. $14,100 D. $10,750

24. What are the total liabilities and capital for Wheelsmith Organic Farms after these transactions have been posted? 24.____

A. $14,100 B. $12,500 C. $11,850 D. $10,600

Questions 25-28.

DIRECTIONS: Questions 25 through 28 are to be answered on the basis of the following information.

At the end of an accounting period, Andy's Framing Gallery recorded the following information: Sales, $125,225; Merchandise Inventory, December 31, $95,325; Purchases Returns and Allowances, $3,500; Merchandise Inventory, January 1, $98,725; Freight on Purchases, $2,500; Purchases, $120,000.

25. What are the net purchases for Andy's Framing Gallery during the accounting period? 25.____

A. $120,000 B. $119,000 C. $3,500 D. $122,500

26. What is the cost of goods available for sale? 26.____

A. $119,000 B. $98,725 C. $95,325 D. $217,725

27. What is the total cost of goods sold for this accounting period? 27.____

A. $217,725 B. $95,325 C. $122,400 D. $125,225

28. What is the gross profit on sales for this accounting period? 28.____

A. $2825 B. $2500 C. $125,225 D. $122,400

Questions 29-40.

DIRECTIONS: Questions 29 through 40 are to be answered on the basis of the following information.

The Joie de Vivre Co. received the promissory notes listed below during the last quarter of its calendar year:

	Date	Face Amount	Terms	Interest Rate	Date Discounted	Discount Rate
(1)	10/8	$3,600	30 days	-	10/18	9%
(2)	9/22	$8,000	60 days	6%	10/1	7%
(3)	11/15	$3,000	90 days	7%	11/20	8%

29. What is the due date for the first note? 29.____

A. 12/31 B. 11/7 C. 12/7 D. 10/31

30. What interest will be due when the first note matures? 30.____

A. $3 B. $3,600 C. $30 D. $0

31. What is the maturity value of the first note? 31.____

A. $3,600 B. $3,630 C. $0 D. $3,603

32. What is the discount period for the first note? 32.____

A. One fiscal year B. 10 days
C. 20 days D. One month

33. What is the due date for the second note? 33.____

A. 12/21 B. 11/21 C. 10/21 D. 1/21

34. What interest will be due when the second note matures? 34.____

A. $60 B. $800.00 C. $8.00 D. $80.00

35. What is the maturity value of the second note? 35.____

A. $8,000 B. $8,080 C. $8,800 D. $8,008

36. What is the discount period for the second note? 36.____

A. 51 days B. 10 days C. 360 days D. 60 days

37. What is the due date for the third note? 37.____

A. 1/14 B. 12/15 C. 12/31 D. 2/13

38. What interest will be due when the third note matures? 38.____

A. $5.25 B. $52.50 C. $525 D. $90

39. What is the maturity value of the third note? 39.____

A. $3525 B. $3005.25 C. $3052.50 D. $3090

40. What is the discount period for the third note? 40.____

A. 60 days B. 85 days C. 5 days D. 90 days

KEY (CORRECT ANSWERS)

1. C	11. C	21. A	31. A
2. A	12. D	22. B	32. C
3. B	13. B	23. C	33. B
4. D	14. B	24. A	34. D
5. C	15. B	25. B	35. B
6. D	16. D	26. D	36. A
7. B	17. C	27. C	37. D
8. A	18. D	28. A	38. B
9. C	19. C	29. B	39. C
10. B	20. D	30. D	40. B

TEST 3

DIRECTIONS: Each question or incomplete statement is followed by several suggested answers or completions. Select the one that BEST answers the question or completes the statement. *PRINT THE LETTER OF THE CORRECT ANSWER IN THE SPACE AT THE RIGHT.*

Questions 1-8.

DIRECTIONS: Questions 1 through 8 are to be answered on the basis of the following Balance Sheet.

Laura Lee's Bridal Shop
Balance Sheet
December 31, 2018

Assets		
Cash	$14,000	
Accounts Receivable	3,000	
Bridal Accessories	10,000	
Gowns and Other Inventory	30,000	
Total Assets		$57,000
Liabilities and Capital		
Accounts Payable	$ 4,000	
Notes Payable	28,000	
Total Liabilities		$32,000
Laura Lee, Capital		25,000
Total Liabilities and Capital		$57,000

1. When was the balance sheet prepared? 1.____

   A. January 2019
   B. December 31, 2018
   C. After the close of the 2018 fiscal year
   D. December 1, 2018

2. How does the date on this balance sheet differ from the date on the statement of capital or income statement? 2.____

   A. It doesn't differ. The dates for each statement signify the same time period.
   B. The date on a balance sheet represents the period during which any changes indicated on the statement took place, whereas the other financial statements represent the moment in time when the statement was prepared.
   C. The date on a balance sheet represents the moment in time when the statement was prepared, whereas the other financial statements represent the period during which any changes indicated on the statement took place.
   D. The date on a balance sheet indicates an entire year, whereas the dates on the other statements indicate a single month.

3. Can Laura Lee purchase more bridal gowns for the business paying cash of $16,000? 3.____

   A. *No*, because the business has only $14,000 cash available
   B. *Yes*, because the business has $57,000 cash available
   C. *Yes*, because the business has $57,000 available in assets
   D. *No*, because the business has $57,000 in liabilities

4. What is the owner's equity of Laura Lee's Bridal Shop? Since total equity consists of total ______, total equity is ______. 4.____

   A. assets minus total liabilities and proprietor's capital; $0
   B. assets minus total liabilities; $25,000
   C. assets; $57,000
   D. liabilities and proprietor's capital; $57,000

5. What is the TOTAL amount of Laura Lee's claim against the total assets of the business? 5.____

   A. $57,000 B. $25,000 C. $0 D. $39,000

6. What is the amount of the creditors' claims against the assets of the business? 6.____

   A. $4,000 B. $57,000 C. $32,000 D. $28,000

7. What is the net income for the period? 7.____

   A. $57,000
   B. $0
   C. $25,000
   D. This information cannot be obtained from the balance sheet

8. What was the value of Laura Lee's ownership in this business on January 1, 2004? 8.____

   A. $25,000
   B. $57,000
   C. $14,000
   D. This information cannot be obtained from the balance sheet

Questions 9-21.

DIRECTIONS: Each of the transactions described in Questions 9 through 21 occurred within an accounting period. For each question, indicate which of the four journals the transaction would be recorded in.

9. Sale of goods on account 9.____

   A. Cash receipts B. Cash payments
   C. General D. Sales

10. Cash payment of a promissory note 10.____

   A. Cash payments B. Cash receipts
   C. Sales D. General

11. Received a credit memo from a creditor 11.____

   A. Purchases B. General
   C. Sales D. Cash payments

12. Sale of merchandise for cash 12.____

   A. Purchases B. General
   C. Cash receipts D. Cash payments

13. Received a check from a customer in partial payment of an oral agreement 13.____

A. Purchases
B. Sales
C. General
D. Cash receipts

14. Issued a credit memo to a customer 14.____

A. Purchases
B. General
C. Cash payments
D. Sales

15. Received a promissory note in place of an oral agreement from a customer 15.____

A. General
B. Cash payments
C. Cash receipts
D. Sales

16. Paid monthly rent 16.____

A. General
B. Purchases
C. Cash payments
D. Cash receipts

17. Sale of a service on credit 17.____

A. Cash receipts
B. General
C. Purchases
D. Sales

18. Purchase of office furniture on credit 18.____

A. General
B. Purchases
C. Cash payments
D. Cash receipts

19. Purchased merchandise for cash 19.____

A. Cash payments
B. Cash receipts
C. Sales
D. General

20. Cash refund to a customer 20.____

A. Cash receipts
B. Sales
C. General
D. Cash payments

21. Purchases made on credit 21.____

A. Purchases
B. Sales
C. Cash receipts
D. General

Questions 22-26.

DIRECTIONS: Questions 22 through 26 are to be answered on the basis of the following inventory, purchased by International Soap and Candle Traders, Inc.

700 units at $4.50, 320 units at $3.75, 550 units at $2.75, and 475 units at $1.90

22. Calculate the total price of the units that cost $4.50. 22.____

A. $315 B. $31,500 C. $3,150 D. $2,800

23. Calculate the total price of the units that cost $3.75. 23.____

A. $2062.50 B. $12,000 C. $120 D. $1,200

24. Calculate the total price of the units that cost $2.75. 24.____

A. $1,512.50 B. $15,125 C. $151.25 D. $550

25. Calculate the total price of the units that cost $1.90. 25.____

A. $90.25 B. $9025 C. $902.50 D. $475

26. Calculate the average cost per unit. 26.____

A. $27 B. $33.10 C. $0.30 D. $3.31

27. The interest on a promissory note is recorded at which of the following times? 27.____

A. When the debt is incurred
B. At the end of the accounting period
C. When the note is paid
D. At the beginning of each month

28. The interest on a promissory note begins accruing at which of the following times? 28.____

A. When the debt is incurred
B. At the end of the accounting period
C. When the note is paid
D. At the beginning of each month

29. The maturity value of an interest-bearing note is the 29.____

A. interest accrued on the note plus a service charge imposed by the lender
B. interest accrued on the note
C. face value of the note
D. principal of the note plus interest

30. A cash receipts journal is used to record the 30.____

A. number of cash sales a business makes
B. number of credit sales a business makes
C. collection of cash made by the business
D. expenditure of cash made by the business

31. Calculate the interest on a promissory note issued for $3,000 at an interest rate of 8%, due in 360 days. (Assume a banking year of 360 days.) 31.____

A. $300 B. $240 C. $60 D. $360

32. Calculate the total payment due for a promissory note issued for $1,000 at an interest rate of 10%, due in 90 days. (Assume a banking year of 360 days.) 32.____

A. $25 B. $1050 C. $1000 D. $1025

33. Calculate the total payment due for a promissory note issued for $5,000 at an interest rate of 6%, due in 60 days. (Assume a banking year of 360 days.) 33.____

A. $5,050 B. $50 C. $5,000 D. $5,300

34. Calculate the interest on a promissory note issued for $1,700 at an interest rate of 12%, due in 45 days. (Assume a banking year of 360 days.) 34.____

A. $204 B. $1725.50 C. $25.50 D. $1904

35. Calculate the interest on a promissory note issued for $600 at an interest rate of 9%, due in 90 days. (Assume a banking year of 360 days.) 35.____

A. $13.50 B. $135 C. $54 D. $540

KEY (CORRECT ANSWERS)

1. B
2. C
3. A
4. B
5. B
6. C
7. D
8. D
9. D
10. A
11. B
12. C
13. D
14. B
15. A
16. C
17. D
18. B
19. A
20. D
21. A
22. C
23. D
24. A
25. C
26. D
27. C
28. A
29. D
30. C
31. B
32. D
33. A
34. C
35. A

EXAMINATION SECTION
TEST 1

DIRECTIONS: Each question or incomplete statement is followed by several suggested answers or completions. Select the one that BEST answers the question or completes the statement. *PRINT THE LETTER OF THE CORRECT ANSWER IN THE SPACE AT THE RIGHT.*

Questions 1 -3

For questions 1 through 3, there is a name or code provided along with four other names or codes listed in alphabetical/numerical order. Find the correct space for the given name or code so that it will be in proper order with the rest of the list.

1. Roggen, Sam 1.____

A. _
Rogers, Arthur L
B. _
Roghani, Fada
C. _
Rogovin, H.T.
D. _
Rogowski, Marie R.
E. _

2. 05076012 2.____

A. _
05076004
B. _
05076007
C. _
05076010
D. _
05076021
E. _

3. CBA-1875 3.____

A. _
CAA-1720
B. _
CAB-1819
C. _
CAC-1804
D. _
CAD-1402
E. _

Questions 4-8

Questions 4 through 8 require you to compare names, addresses or codes. In each line below there are three items that are very much alike. Compare the three and answer as follows:

Answer "A" if all three are exactly alike;
Answer "B" if only the FIRST and SECOND items are exactly alike;
Answer "C" if only the FIRST and THIRD items are exactly alike;
Answer "D" if only the SECOND AND THIRD items are exactly alike;
Answer "E" if all three names are different.

4.	Helene Bedell	Helene Beddell	Helene Beddell	4.___
5.	FT. Wedemeyer	FT. Wedemeyer	FT. Wedmeyer	5.___
6.	3214 W. Beaumont St.	3214 W. Beaumount St.	3214 Beaumont St.	6.___
7.	BC3105T-5	BC3015T-5	BC3105T-5	7.___
8.	4460327	4460327	4460327	8.___

For questions 9 through 11, find the correct spelling of the word and write the correct letter in the space at the right.

9. A. accomodate B. acommodate C. accommadate D. none of the above 9.___

10. A. manageble B. manageable C. manegeable D. none of the above 10.___

11. A. reccommend B. recommend C. recammend D. none of the above 11.___

12. 32 + 26 = 12.___

A. 69
B. 59
C. 58
D. 54
E. none of the above

13. 57-15 = 13.___

A. 72
B. 62
C. 54
D. 44
E. none of the above

14. 23x7 = 14.___

A. 164
B. 161
C. 154
D. 141
E. none of the above

15. 160/5 = 15.___

A. 32

B. 30
C. 25
D. 21
E. none of the above

16. 17.8 + 13.3 = 16.____

A. 30.1
B. 31.0
C. 31.1
D. 33.3

Questions 17-19

Questions 17 through 19 test the ability to follow instructions. Following the directions in each item will lead you to identify or create a specific letter-number combination. Next, use the "Look-Up Table" to find the letter that corresponds with your letter-number combination. Mark this letter in the space at the right.

For example, if the combination is "P1," the answer would be "A" because this is the letter indicated in the box where "P" and "1" meet in the table.

LOOK-UP TABLE					
	P	Q	R	S	T
1	A	B	C	D	E
2	B	C	D	E	A
3	C	D	E	A	B
4	D	E	A	B	C
5	E	A	B	C	D
6	A	B	C	D	E
7	B	C	D	E	A
8	C	D	E	A	B
9	D	E	A	B	C
10	E	A	B	C	D

17. Look at the letter-number combinations below. Draw a circle around the third combination from the left. Write that letter-number combination in this space: ______ 17.____

T1 S5 P2 Q5 P5 R2

18. Draw a line under each letter that appears only once in the line. Write the letter "Q" and the number of lines you drew here: ______ 18.____

S T Q T Q P T Q

19. Look again at the line of letters in question 16. Draw a circle around each "Q." Write the letter that appears at the beginning of the line and the number of circles you drew here: 19.____

______

20. Select the sentence which is MOST APPROPRIATE with respect to grammar, usage and punctuation suitable for a formal letter or report: 20.____

A. Major repairs has caused the cafeteria to be closed until late October.
B. The cafeteria will be closed until late October on account of major repairs.

C. The cafeteria will be closed for major repairs until late October.
D. The closing of the cafeteria until late October due to the completion of major repairs.

In questions 21 through 23, identify the most similar meaning to the highlighted word:

21. The staff was **amazed** by the news. 21.___

A. pleased
B. surprised
C. saddened
D. relieved

22. Please **delete** the second paragraph. 22.___

A. retype
B. reread
C. revise
D. remove

23. Did you **duplicate** the information as written? 23.___

A. type
B. copy
C. remember
D. understand

24. "It is a simple matter to find and correct the errors made by a typist, but often a file clerk's errors are not discovered until something which is needed cannot be found. For this reason, the work of every file clerk should be checked at regular intervals." 24.___
The paragraph BEST supports the statement that filing

A. may contain errors that are not immediately noticeable
B. should be organized by typists rather than file clerks
C. is a more difficult process than typing
D. should be checked for errors more frequently than typing

25. "The most efficient method for performing a task is not always easily determined. That which is economical in terms of time must be carefully distinguished from that which is economical in terms of expended energy. In short, the quickest method may require a degree of physical effort that may be neither essential nor desirable." The paragraph BEST supports the statement that 25.___

A. it is more efficient to perform a task slowly than rapidly
B. skill in performing a task should not be acquired at the expense of time
C. the most efficient execution of a task is not always the one done in the shortest time
D. energy and time cannot both be considered in the performance of a single task

KEY (CORRECT ANSWERS)

1. B
2. D
3. E
4. D
5. B

6. E
7. C
8. A
9. D
10. B

11. B
12. C
13. E
14. B
15. A

16. C
17. B
18. C
19. A
20. C

21. B
22. D
23. B
24. A
25. C

CLERICAL ABILITIES

EXAMINATION SECTION

TEST 1

DIRECTIONS: Each question or incomplete statement is followed by several suggested answers or completions. Select the one that BEST answers the question or completes the statement. *PRINT THE LETTER OF THE CORRECT ANSWER IN THE SPACE AT THE RIGHT.*

Questions 1-4.

DIRECTIONS: Questions 1 through 4 are to be answered on the basis of the information given below.

The most commonly used filing system and the one that is easiest to learn is alphabetical filing. This involves putting records in an A to Z order, according to the letters of the alphabet. The name of a person is filed by using the following order: first, the surname or last name; second, the first name; third, the middle name or middle initial. For example, *Henry C. Young* is filed under *Y* and thereafter under *Young, Henry C.* The name of a company is filed in the same way. For example, *Long Cabinet Co.* is filed under *L* while *John T. Long Cabinet Co.* is filed under *L* and thereafter under *Long, John T. Cabinet Co.*

1. The one of the following which lists the names of persons in the CORRECT alphabetical order is: 1.____
   A. Mary Carrie, Helen Carrol, James Carson, John Carter
   B. James Carson, Mary Carrie, John Carter, Helen Carrol
   C. Helen Carrol, James Carson, John Carter, Mary Carrie
   D. John Carter, Helen Carrol, Mary Carrie, James Carson

2. The one of the following which lists the names of persons in the CORRECT alphabetical order is: 2.____
   A. Jones, John C.; Jones, John A.; Jones, John P.; Jones, John K.
   B. Jones, John P.; Jones, John K.; Jones, John C.; Jones, John A.
   C. Jones, John A.; Jones, John C.; Jones, John K.; Jones, John P.
   D. Jones, John K.; Jones, John C.; Jones, John A.; Jones, John P.

3. The one of the following which lists the names of the companies in the CORRECT alphabetical order is: 3.____
   A. Blane Co., Blake Co., Block Co., Blear Co.
   B. Blake Co., Blane Co., Blear Co., Block Co.
   C. Block Co., Blear Co., Blane Co., Blake Co.
   D. Blear Co., Blake Co., Blane Co., Block Co.

4. You are to return to the file an index card on *Barry C. Wayne Materials and Supplies Co.* 4.____
Of the following, the CORRECT alphabetical group that you should return the index card to is
A. A to G B. H to M C. N to S D. T to Z

Questions 5-10.

DIRECTIONS: In each of Questions 5 through 10, the names of four people are given. For each question, choose as your answer the one of the four names given which should be filed FIRST according to the usual system of alphabetical filing of names, as described in the following paragraph.

In filing names, you must start with the last name. Names are filed in order of the first letter of the last name, then the second letter, etc. Therefore, BAILY would be filed before BROWN, which would be filed before COLT. A name with fewer letters of the same type comes first, i.e., Smith before Smithe. If the last names are the same, the names are filed alphabetically by the first name. If the first name is an initial, a name with an initial would come before a first name that starts with the same letter as the initial. Therefore, I. BROWN would come before IRA BROWN. Finally, if both last name and first name are the same, the name would be filed alphabetically by the middle name, once again an initial coming before a middle name which starts with the same letter as the initial. If there is no middle name at all, the name would come before those with middle initials or names.

SAMPLE QUESTION:
A. Lester Daniels
B. William Dancer
C. Nathan Danzig
D. Dan Lester

The last names beginning with D are filed before the last name beginning with L. Since DANIELS, DANCER, and DANZIG all begin with the same three letters, you must look at the fourth letter of the last name to determine which name should be filed first. C comes before I or Z in the alphabet, so DANCER is filed before DANIELS or DANZIG. Therefore, the answer to the above sample question is B.

5. 5.____
A. Scott Biala
B. Mary Byala
C. Martin Baylor
D. Francis Bauer

6. 6.____
A. Howard J. Black
B. Howard Black
C. J. Howard Black
D. John H. Black

7. 7.____
A. Theodora Garth Kingston
B. Theadore Barth Kingston
C. Thomas Kingston
D. Thomas T. Kingston

8. A. Paulette Mary Huerta 8.____
   B. Paul M. Huerta
   C. Paulette L. Huerta
   D. Peter A. Huerta

9. A. Martha Hunt Morgan 9.____
   B. Martin Hunt Morgan
   C. Mary H. Morgan
   D. Martine H. Morgan

10. A. James T. Meerschaum 10.____
    B. James M. Mershum
    C. James F. Mearshaum
    D. James N. Meshum

Questions 11-14.

DIRECTIONS: Questions 11 through 14 are to be answered SOLELY on the basis of the following information.

You are required to file various documents in file drawers which are labeled according to the following pattern:

DOCUMENTS

MEMOS		LETTERS	
File	Subject	File	Subject
84PM1	(A-L)	84PC1	(A-L)
84PM2	(M-Z)	84PC2	(M-Z)

REPORTS		INQUIRIES	
File	Subject	File	Subject
84PR1	(A-L)	84PQ1	(A-L)
84PR2	(M-Z)	84PQ2	(M-Z)

11. A letter dealing with a burglary should be filed in the drawer labeled 11.____
    A. 84PM1 B. 84PC1 C. 84PR1 D. 84PQ2

12. A report on Statistics should be found in the drawer labeled 12.____
    A. 84PM1 B. 84PC2 C. 84PR2 D. 84PQS

13. An inquiry is received about parade permit procedures. It should be filed in the drawer labeled 13.____
    A. 84PM2 B. 84PC1 C. 84PR1 D. 84PQ2

14. A police officer has a question about a robbery report you filed. You should pull this file from the drawer labeled 14.____
    A. 84PM1 B. 84PM2 C. 84PR1 D. 84PR2

Questions 15-22.

DIRECTIONS: Each of Questions 15 through 22 consists of four or six numbered names. For each question, choose the option (A, B, C, or D) which indicates the order in which the names should be filed in accordance with the following filing instructions:

- File alphabetically according to last name, then first name, then middle initial.
- File according to each successive letter within a name.
- When comparing two names in which the letters in the longer name are identical to the corresponding letters in the shorter name, the shorter name is filed first.
- When the last names are the same, initials are always filed before names beginning with the same letter.

15. I. Ralph Robinson 15.____
    II. Alfred Ross
    III. Luis Robles
    IV. James Roberts

    The CORRECT filing sequence for the above names should be
    A. IV, II, I, III B. I, IV, III, II C. III, IV, I, II D. IV, I, III, II

16. I. Irwin Goodwin 16.____
    II. Inez Gonzalez
    III. Irene Goodman
    IV. Ira S. Goodwin
    V. Ruth I. Goldstein
    VI. M.B. Goodman

    The CORRECT filing sequence for the above names should be
    A. V, II, I, IV, III, VI B. V, II, VI, III, IV, I
    C. V, II, III, VI, IV, I D. V, II, III, VI, I, IV

17. I. George Allan 17.____
    II. Gregory Allen
    III. Gary Allen
    IV. George Allen

    The CORRECT filing sequence for the above names should be
    A. IV, III, I, II B. I, IV, II, III C. III, IV, I, II D. I, III, IV, II

18. I. Simon Kauffman 18.____
    II. Leo Kaufman
    III. Robert Kaufmann
    IV. Paul Kauffmann

    The CORRECT filing sequence for the above names should be
    A. I, IV, II, III B. II, IV, III, I C. III, II, IV, I D. I, II, III, IV

19. I. Roberta Williams 19.____
    II. Robin Wilson
    III. Roberta Wilson
    IV. Robin Williams

    The CORRECT filing sequence for the above names should be
    A. III, II, IV, I B. I, IV, III, II C. I, II, III, IV D. III, I, II, IV

20. I. Lawrence Shultz 20.____
    II. Albert Schultz
    III. Theodore Schwartz
    IV. Thomas Schwarz
    V. Alvin Schultz
    VI. Leonard Shultz

    The CORRECT filing sequence for the above names should be
    A. II, V, III, IV, I, VI B. IV, III, V, I, II, VI
    C. II, V, I, VI, III, IV D. I, VI, II, V, III, IV

21. I. McArdle 21.____
    II. Mayer
    III. Maletz
    IV. McNiff
    V. Meyer
    VI. MacMahon

    The CORRECT filing sequence for the above names should be
    A. I, IV, VI, III, II, V B. II, I, IV, VI, III, V
    C. VI, III, II, I, IV, V D. VI, III, II, V, I, IV

22. I. Jack E. Johnson 22.____
    II. R.H. Jackson
    III. Bertha Jackson
    IV. J.T. Johnson
    V. Ann Johns
    VI. John Jacobs

    The CORRECT filing sequence for the above names should be
    A. II, III, VI, V, IV, I B. III, II, VI, V, IV, I
    C. VI, II, III, I, V, IV D. III, II, VI, IV, V, I

Questions 23-30.

DIRECTIONS: The code table below shows 10 letters with matching numbers. For each question, there are three sets of letters. Each set of letters is followed by a set of numbers which may or may not match their correct letter according to the code table. For each question, check all three sets of letters and numbers and mark your answer:

A. if no pairs are correctly matched
B. if only one pair is correctly matched
C. if only two pairs are correctly matched
D. if all three pairs are correctly matched

CODE TABLE

T	M	V	D	S	P	R	G	B	H
1	2	3	4	5	6	7	8	9	0

SAMPLE QUESTION: TMVDSP – 123456
RGBHTM – 789011
DSPRGB – 256789

In the sample question above, the first set of numbers correctly match its set of letters. But the second and third pairs contain mistakes. In the second pair, M is correctly matched with number 1. According to the code table, letter M should be correctly matched with number 2. In the third pair, the letter D is incorrectly matched with number 2. According to the code table, letter D should be correctly matched with number 4. Since only one of the pairs is correctly matched, the answer to this sample question is B.

23. RSBMRM – 759262 23.____
GDSRVH – 845730
VDBRTM - 349713

24. TGVSDR – 183247 24.____
SMHRDP – 520647
TRMHSR - 172057

25. DSPRGM – 456782 25.____
MVDBHT – 234902
HPMDBT - 062491

26. BVPTRD – 936184 26.____
GDPHMB – 807029
GMRHMV - 827032

27. MGVRSH – 283750 27.____
TRDMBS – 174295
SPRMGV - 567283

28. SGBSDM – 489542 28.____
MGHPTM – 290612
MPBMHT - 269301

29. TDPBHM – 146902 29.____
VPBMRS – 369275
GDMBHM - 842902

30. MVPTBV – 236194 30.____
PDRTMB – 47128
BGTMSM - 981232

KEY (CORRECT ANSWERS)

1.	A	11.	B	21.	C
2.	C	12.	C	22.	B
3.	B	13.	D	23.	B
4.	D	14.	D	24.	B
5.	D	15.	D	25.	C
6.	B	16.	C	26.	A
7.	B	17.	D	27.	D
8.	B	18.	A	28.	A
9.	A	19.	B	29.	D
10.	C	20.	A	30.	A

TEST 2

DIRECTIONS: Each question or incomplete statement is followed by several suggested answers or completions. Select the one that BEST answers the question or completes the statement. *PRINT THE LETTER OF THE CORRECT ANSWER IN THE SPACE AT THE RIGHT.*

Questions 1-10.

DIRECTIONS: Questions 1 through 10 each consists of two columns, each containing four lines of names, numbers and/or addresses. For each question, compare the lines in Column I with the lines in Column II to see if they match exactly, and mark your answer A, B, C, or D, according to the following instructions:

A. all four lines match exactly
B. only three lines match exactly
C. only two lines match exactly
D. only one line matches exactly

		COLUMN I	COLUMN II	
1.	I.	Earl Hodgson	Earl Hodgson	1.____
	II.	1409870	1408970	
	III.	Shore Ave.	Schore Ave.	
	IV.	Macon Rd.	Macon Rd.	
2.	I.	9671485	9671485	2.____
	II.	470 Astor Court	470 Astor Court	
	III.	Halprin, Phillip	Halperin, Phillip	
	IV.	Frank D. Poliseo	Frank D. Poliseo	
3.	I.	Tandem Associates	Tandom Associates	3.____
	II.	144-17 Northern Blvd.	144-17 Northern Blvd.	
	III.	Alberta Forchi	Albert Forchi	
	IV.	Kings Park, NY 10751	Kings Point, NY 10751	
4.	I.	Bertha C. McCormack	Bertha C. McCormack	4.____
	II.	Clayton, MO	Clayton, MO	
	III.	976-4242	976-4242	
	IV.	New City, NY 10951	New City, NY 10951	
5.	I.	George C. Morill	George C. Morrill	5.____
	II.	Columbia, SC 29201	Columbia, SD 29201	
	III.	Louis Ingham	Louis Ingham	
	IV.	3406 Forest Ave.	3406 Forest Ave.	
6.	I.	506 S. Elliott Pl.	506 S. Elliott Pl.	6.____
	II.	Herbert Hall	Hurbert Hall	
	III.	4712 Rockaway Pkway	4712 Rockaway Pkway	
	IV.	169 E. 7 St.	169 E. 7 St.	

7.	I.	345 Park Ave.	345 Park Pl.	7.____
	II.	Colman Oven Corp.	Coleman Oven Corp.	
	III.	Robert Conte	Robert Conti	
	IV.	6179846	6179846	
8.	I.	Grigori Schierber	Grigori Schierber	8.____
	II.	Des Moines, Iowa	Des Moines, Iowa	
	III.	Gouverneur Hospital	Gouverneur Hospital	
	IV.	91-35 Cresskill Pl.	91-35 Cresskill Pl.	
9.	I.	Jeffery Janssen	Jeffrey Janssen	9.____
	II.	8041071	8041071	
	III.	40 Rockefeller Plaza	40 Rockafeller Plaza	
	IV.	407 6 St.	406 7 St.	
10.	I.	5971996	5871996	10.____
	II.	3113 Knickerbocker Ave.	31123 Knickerbocker Ave.	
	III.	8434 Boston Post Rd.	8424 Boston Post Rd.	
	IV.	Penn Station	Penn Station	

Questions 11-14.

DIRECTIONS: Questions 11 through 14 are to be answered by looking at the four groups of names and addresses listed below (I, II, III, and IV), and then finding out the number of groups that have their corresponding numbered lies exactly the same.

	GROUP I	GROUP II
Line 1.	Richmond General Hospital	Richman General Hospital
Line 2.	Geriatric Clinic	Geriatric Clinic
Line 3.	3975 Paerdegat St.	3975 Peardegat St.
Line 4.	Loudonville, New York 11538	Londonville, New York 11538

	GROUP III	GROUP IV
Line 1.	Richmond General Hospital	Richmend General Hospital
Line 2.	Geriatric Clinic	Geriatric Clinic
Line 3.	3795 Paerdegat St.	3975 Paerdegat St.
Line 4.	Loudonville, New York 11358	Loudonville, New York 11538

1. In how many groups is line one exactly the same? 11.____
   A. Two B. Three C. Four D. None

12. In how many groups is line two exactly the same? 12.____
    A. Two B. Three C. Four D. None

13. In how many groups is line three exactly the same? 13.____
    A. Two B. Three C. Four D. None

14. In how many groups is line four exactly the same? 14.____
A. Two B. Three C. Four D. None

Questions 15-18.

DIRECTIONS: Each of Questions 15 through 18 has two lists of names and addresses. Each list contains three sets of names and addresses. Check each of the three sets in the list on the right to see if they are the same as the corresponding set in the list on the left. Mark your answers:
A. if none of the sets in the right list are the same as those in the left list
B. if only one of the sets in the right list is the same as those in the left list
C. if only two of the sets in the right list are the same as those in the left list
D. if all three sets in the right list are the same as those in the left list

15.	Mary T. Berlinger 2351 Hampton St. Monsey, N.Y. 20117	Mary T. Berlinger 2351 Hampton St. Monsey, N.Y. 20117	15.____
	Eduardo Benes 483 Kingston Avenue Central Islip, N.Y. 11734	Eduardo Benes 473 Kingston Avenue Central Islip, N.Y. 11734	
	Alan Carrington Fuchs 17 Gnarled Hollow Road Los Angeles, CA 91635	Alan Carrington Fuchs 17 Gnarled Hollow Road Los Angeles, CA 91685	
16.	David John Jacobson 178 34 St. Apt. 4C New York, N.Y. 00927	David John Jacobson 178 53 St. Apt. 4C New York, N.Y. 00927	16.____
	Ann-Marie Calonella 7243 South Ridge Blvd. Bakersfield, CA 96714	Ann-Marie Calonella 7243 South Ridge Blvd. Bakersfield, CA 96714	
	Pauline M. Thompson 872 Linden Ave. Houston, Texas 70321	Pauline M. Thomson 872 Linden Ave. Houston, Texas 70321	
17.	Chester LeRoy Masterton 152 Lacy Rd. Kankakee, Ill. 54532	Chester LeRoy Masterson 152 Lacy Rd. Kankakee, Ill. 54532	17.____
	William Maloney S. LaCrosse Pla. Wausau, Wisconsin 52136	William Maloney S. LaCross Pla. Wausau, Wisconsin 52146	
	Cynthia V. Barnes 16 Pines Rd. Greenpoint, Miss. 20376	Cynthia V. Barnes 16 Pines Rd. Greenpoint,, Miss. 20376	

18.	Marcel Jean Frontenac 8 Burton On The Water Calender, Me. 01471	Marcel Jean Frontenac 6 Burton On The Water Calender, Me. 01471	18.____
	J. Scott Marsden 174 S. Tipton St. Cleveland, Ohio	J. Scott Marsden 174 Tipton St. Cleveland, Ohio	
	Lawrence T. Haney 171 McDonough St. Decatur, Ga. 31304	Lawrence T. Haney 171 McDonough St. Decatur, Ga. 31304	

Questions 19-26.

DIRECTIONS: Each of Questions 19 through 26 has two lists of numbers. Each list contains three sets of numbers. Check each of the three sets in the list on the right to see if they are the same as the corresponding set in the list on the left. Mark your answers:

A. if none of the sets in the right list are the same as those in the left list
B. if only one of the sets in the right list is the same as those in the left list
C. if only two of the sets in the right list are the same as those in the left list
D. if all three sets in the right list are the same as those in the left lists

19.	7354183476 4474747744 5791430231	7354983476 4474747774 57914302311	19.____
20.	7143592185 8344517699 9178531263	7143892185 8344518699 9178531263	20.____
21.	2572114731 8806835476 8255831246	257214731 8806835476 8255831246	21.____
22.	331476853821 6976658532996 3766042113715	331476858621 6976655832996 3766042113745	22.____
23.	8806663315 74477138449 211756663666	88066633115 74477138449 211756663666	23.____

24. 990006966996 53022219743 4171171117717	99000696996 53022219843 4171171177717	24.____
25. 24400222433004 5300030055000355 20000075532002022	24400222433004 5300030055500355 20000075532002022	25.____
26. 611166640660001116 7111300117001100733 26666446664476518	61116664066001116 7111300117001100733 26666446664476518	26.____

Questions 27-30.

DIRECTIONS: Questions 27 through 30 are to be answered by picking the answer which is in the correct numerical order, from the lowest number to the highest number, in each question.

27. A. 44533, 44518, 44516, 44547 27.____
B. 44516, 44518, 44533, 44547
C. 44547, 44533, 44518, 44516
D. 44518, 44516, 44547, 44533

28. A. 95587, 95593, 95601, 95620 28.____
B. 95601, 95620, 95587, 95593
C. 95593, 95587, 95601. 95620
D. 95620, 95601, 95593, 95587

29. A. 232212, 232208, 232232, 232223 29.____
B. 232208, 232223, 232212, 232232
C. 232208, 232212, 232223, 232232
D. 232223, 232232, 232208, 232208

30. A. 113419, 113521, 113462, 113462 30.____
B. 113588, 113462, 113521, 113419
C. 113521, 113588, 113419, 113462
D. 113419, 113462, 113521, 113588

KEY (CORRECT ANSWERS)

1.	C	11.	A	21.	C
2.	B	12.	C	22.	A
3.	D	13.	A	23.	D
4.	A	14.	A	24.	A
5.	C	15.	C	25.	C
6.	B	16.	B	26.	C
7.	D	17.	B	27.	B
8.	A	18.	B	28.	A
9.	D	19.	B	29.	C
10.	C	20.	B	30.	D

FILING

EXAMINATION SECTION

TEST 1

Questions 1-9.

DIRECTIONS: An important part of the duties of an office worker in a public agency is to file office records. Questions 1 through 9 are designed to determine whether you can file records correctly. Each of these questions consists of four names. For each question, select the one of the four names that should be FOURTH if the four names were arranged in alphabetical order. *PRINT THE LETTER OF THE CORRECT ANSWER IN THE SPACE AT THE RIGHT.*

1. A. 6th National Bank B. Sexton Lock Co. 1.____
   C. The 69th Street League D. Thomas Saxon Corp.

2. A. 4th Avenue Printing Co. B. The Four Corners Corp. 2.____
   C. Dr. Milton Fournet D. The Martin Fountaine Co.

3. A. Mr. Chas. Le Mond B. Model Express, Inc. 3.____
   C. Lenox Enterprises D. Mobile Supply Co.

4. A. Frank Waller Johnson B. Frank Walter Johnson 4.____
   C. Wilson Johnson D. Frank W. Johnson

5. A. Miss Anne M. Carlsen B. Mrs. Albert S. Carlson 5.____
   C. Mr. Alan Ross Carlsen D. Dr. Anthony Ash Carlson

6. A. Delaware Paper Co. B. William Del Ville 6.____
   C. Ralph A. Delmar D. Wm. K. Del Ville

7. A. The Lloyd Disney Co. B. Mrs. Raymond Norris 7.____
   C. Oklahoma Envelope, Inc. D. Miss Esther O'Neill

8. A. The Olympic Eraser Co. B. Mrs. Raymond Norris 8.____
   C. Oklahoma Envelope, Inc. D. Miss Esther O'Neill

9. A. Patricia MacNamara B. Eleanor McNally 9.____
   C. Robt. MacPherson, Jr. D. Helen McNair

Questions 10-21.

DIRECTIONS: Questions 10 through 21 are to be answered on the basis of the usual rules for alphabetical filing. For each question, indicate in the space at the right the letter preceding the name which should be THIRD in alphabetical order.

10. A. Russell Cohen B. Henry Cohn 10.____
C. Wesley Chambers D. Arthur Connors

11. A. Wanda Jenkins B. Pauline Jennings 11.____
C. Leslie Jantzenberg D. Rudy Jensen

12. A. Arnold Wilson B. Carlton Willson 12.____
C. Duncan Williamson D. Ezra Wilston

13. A. Joseph M. Buchman B. Gustave Bozzerman 13.____
C. Constantino Brunelli D. Armando Buccino

14. A. Barbara Waverly B. Corinne Warterdam 14.____
C. Dennis Waterman D. Harold Wartman

15. A. Jose Mejia B. Bernard Mendelsohn 15.____
C. Antonio Mejias D. Richard Mazzitelli

16. A. Hesselberg, Norman J. B. Hesselman, Nathan B. 16.____
C. Hazel, Robert S. D. Heintz, August J.

17. A. Oshins, Jerome B. Ohsie, Marjorie 17.____
C. O'Shaugn, F.J. D. O'Shea, Frances

18. A. Petrie, Joshua A. B. Pendleton, Oscar 18.____
C. Pertwee, Joshua D. Perkins, Warren G.

19. A. Morganstern, Alfred B. Morganstern, Albert 19.____
C. Monroe, Mildred D. Modesti, Ernest

20. A. More, Stewart B. Moorhead, Jay 20.____
C. Moore, Benjamin D. Moffat, Edith

21. A. Ramirez, Paul B. Revere, Pauline 21.____
C. Ramos, Felix D. Ramazotti, Angelo

KEY (CORRECT ANSWERS)

1.	C	11.	B
2.	A	12.	A
3.	B	13.	D
4.	B	14.	C
5.	D	15.	C
6.	A	16.	A
7.	C	17.	D
8.	D	18.	C
9.	B	19.	B
10.	B	20.	B

21. C

TEST 2

DIRECTIONS: Each question or incomplete statement is followed by several suggested answers or completions. Select the one that BEST answers the question or completes the statement. *PRINT THE LETTER OF THE CORRECT ANSWER IN THE SPACE AT THE RIGHT.*

Questions 1-4.

DIRECTIONS: Questions 1 through 4 are to be answered on the basis of the following alphabetical rules.

RULES FOR ALPHABETICAL FILING

<u>Names of Individuals</u>

The names of individuals are filed in strict alphabetical order, *first* according to the last name, *then* according to first name or initial, and *finally* according to middle name or initial. For example: George Allen precedes Edward Bell and Leonard Reston precedes Lucille Reston.

When last names are the same, for example, A. Green and Agnes Green, the one with the initial comes before the one with the name written out when the first initials are identical.

Prefixes such as De, O', Mac, Mc and Van are filed as written and are treated as part of the names to which they are connected. For example, Gladys McTeaque is filed before Frances Meadows.

1. If the following four names were put into an alphabetical list, what would the FIRST name on the list be? 1.____
   A. Wm. C. Paul
   B. W. Paul
   C. Alice Paul
   D. Alyce Paule

2. If the following four names were put into an alphabetical list, what would the THIRD name on the list be? 2.____
   A. I. MacCarthy
   B. Irene MacKarthy
   C. Ida McCaren
   D. I.A. McCarthy

3. If the following four names were put into an alphabetical list, what would the SECOND name on the list be? 3.____
   A. John Gilhooley
   B. Ramon Gonzalez
   C. Gerald Gilholy
   D. Samuel Gilvecchio

4. If the following four names were put into an alphabetical list, what would the FOURTH name on the list be? 4.____
   A. Michael Edwinn
   B. James Edwards
   C. Mary Edwin
   D. Carlo Edwards

Questions 5-9.

DIRECTIONS: Questions 5 through 9 consist of a group of names which are to be arranged in alphabetical order for filing.

5. Of the following, the name which should be filed FIRST is 5.____
   A. Joseph J. Meadeen
   B. Gerard L. Meader
   C. John F. Madcar
   D. Philip F. Malder

6. Of the following, the name which should be filed LAST is 6.____
   A. Stephen Fischer
   B. Benjamin Fitchmann
   C. Thomas Fishman
   D. Augustus S. Fisher

7. The name which should be filed SECOND is 7.____
   A. Yeatman, Frances
   B. Yeaton, C.S.
   C. Yeatman, R.M.
   D. Yeats, John

8. The name which should be filed THIRD is 8.____
   A. Hauser, Ann
   B. Hauptmann, Jane
   C. Hauster, Mary
   D. Rauprich, Julia

9. The name which should be filed SECOND is 9.____
   A. Flora McDougall
   B. Fred E. MacDowell
   C. Juanita Mendez
   D. James A. Madden

Questions 10-14.

DIRECTIONS: Questions 10 through 14 are to be answered based on an alphabetical arrangement of the following list of names.

Walker, Carol J.	Wacht, Michael	Wade, Ethel
Wall, Fredrick	Wall, Francis	Wall, Frank
Wachs, Paul	Walker, Carol L.	Wagner, Arthur
Walters, Daniel	Wade, Ellen	Wald, William
Wagner, Allen	Walters, David	Walker, Carmen

10. The 4th name on the alphabetized list would be 10.____
   A. Wade, Ellen
   B. Wade, Ethel
   C. Wagner, Allen
   D. Wagner, Arthur

11. The 7th name on the alphabetized list would be 11.____
   A. Walker, Carmen
   B. Walker, Carol J.
   C. Walker, Carol L.
   D. Wald, William

12. The name that would come immediately AFTER Wagner, Arthur on the alphabetized list would be 12.____
   A. Wade, Ethel
   B. Wagner, Allen
   C. Wald, William
   D. Walker, Carol L.

13. The name that would come immediately BEFORE Wall, Frank would be 13.____
   A. Wall, Francis
   B. Wall, Fredrick
   C. Walters, David
   D. Walters, Daniel

14. The 12th name on the alphabetized list would be 14.____
   A. Walker, Carol L.
   B. Wald, William
   C. Wall, Francis
   D. Wall, Frank

KEY (CORRECT ANSWERS)

1.	C	6.	B	11.	D
2.	C	7.	C	12.	C
3.	A	8.	A	13.	A
4.	A	9.	D	14.	D
5.	C	10.	B		

TEST 3

DIRECTIONS: Each question or incomplete statement is followed by several suggested answers or completions. Select the one that BEST answers the question or completes the statement. *PRINT THE LETTER OF THE CORRECT ANSWER IN THE SPACE AT THE RIGHT.*

Questions 1-8.

DIRECTIONS: Questions 1 through 8 are based on the Rules of Alphabetical Filing given below. Read these rules carefully before answering the questions.

Names of People

1. The names of people are filed in strict alphabetical order, first according to the last name, then according to first name or initial, and finally according to middle name or initial. For example: George Allen comes before Edward Bell, and Leonard P. Reston comes before Lucille B. Reston.

2. When last names are the same, for example, A. Green and Agnes Green, the one with the initial comes before the one with the name written out when the first initials are identical.

3. When first and last names are alike and the middle name is given, for example, John David Doe and John Devoe Doe, the names should be filed in alphabetical order of the middle names.

4. When first and last names are the same, a name without a middle initial comes before one with a middle name or initial. For example, John Doe comes before John A. Doe and John Alan Doe.

5. When first and last names are the same, a name with a middle initial comes before one with a middle name beginning with the same initial. For example, Jack R. Hertz comes before Jack Richard Hertz.

6. Prefixes such as De, O', Mac, Mc, and Van are filed as written and are treated as part of the names to which they are connected. For example, Robert O'Dea is filed before David Olsen.

7. Abbreviated names are treated as if they were spelled out. For example: Chas. is filed as Charles and Thos. is filed as Thomas.

8. Titles and designations such as Dr., Mr., and Prof. are disregarded in filing.

Names of Organizations

1. The names of business organizations are filed according to the order in which each word in the name appears. When an organization name bears the name of a person, it is filed according to the rules for filing names of people as given above. For example: William Smith Service Co. comes before Television Distributors, Inc.

2. Where bureau, board, office or department appears as the first part of the title of a governmental agency, that agency should be filed under the word in the title expressing the chief function of the agency. For example, Bureau of Budget would be filed as if written Budget, (Bureau of the). The Department of Personnel would be filed as if written Personnel, (Department of).

3. When the following words are part of an organization, they are disregarded: the, of, and.

4. When there are numbers in a name, they are treated as if they were spelled out. For example: 10th Street Bootery is filed as Tenth Street Bootery.

Each question from 1 through 8 contains four names numbered from 1 through 4 but not necessarily numbered in correct filing order. Answer each question by choosing the letter corresponding to the CORRECT filing order of the four names in accordance with the above rules.

SAMPLE QUESTION:
I. Robert J. Smith
II. R. Jeffrey Smith
III. Dr. A. Smythe
IV. Allen R. Smithers

A. I, II, III, IV B. III, I, II, IV C. II, I, IV, III D. III, II, I, IV

Since the correct filing order, in accordance with the above rules is II I, IV, III, the correct answer is C.

1. I. J. Chester VanClief II. John C. Van Clief 1.____
III. J. VanCleve IV. Mary L. Vance

The CORRECT answer is:
A. IV, III, I, II B. IV, III, II, I C. III, I, II, IV D. III, IV, I, II

2. I. Community Development Agency II. Department of Social Services 2.____
III. Board of Estimate IV. Bureau of Gas and Electricity

The CORRECT answer is:
A. III, IV, I, II B. 1, II, IV, III C. II, I, III, IV D. I, III, IV, II

3. I. Dr. Chas. K. Dahlman II. F. & A. Delivery Service 3.____
III. Department of Water Supply IV. Demano Men's Custom Tailors

The CORRECT answer is:
A. I, II, III, IV B. I, IV, II, III C. IV, I, II, III D. IV, I, III, II

4. I. 48th Street Theater II. Fourteenth Street Day Care Center 4.____
III. Professor A. Cartwright IV. Albert F. McCarthy

The CORRECT answer is:
A. IV, II, I, III B. IV, III, I, II C. III, II, I, IV D. III, I, II, IV

5. I. Frances D'Arcy II. Mario L. DelAmato 5.____
III. William R. Diamond IV. Robert J. DuBarry

The CORRECT answer is:
A. I, II, IV, III B. II, I, III, IV C. I, II, III, IV D. II, I, III, IV

6. I. Evelyn H. D'Amelio II. Jane R. Bailey 6.____
III. Robert Bailey IV. Frank Baily

The CORRECT answer is:
A. I, II, III, IV B. I, III, II, IV C. II, III, IV, I D. III, II, IV, I

7. I. Department of Markets 7.____
II. Bureau of Handicapped Children
III. Housing Authority Administration Building
IV. Board of Pharmacy

The CORRECT answer is:
A. II, I, III, IV B. I, II, IV, III C. I, II, III, IV D. III, II, I, IV

8. I. William A. Shea Stadium II. Rapid Speed Taxi Co. 8.____
III. Harry Stampler's Rotisserie III. Wilhelm Albert Shea

The CORRECT answer is:
A. II, III, IV, I B. IV, I, III, II C. II, IV, I, III D. III, IV, I, II

Questions 9-18.

DIRECTIONS: Questions 9 through 18 each show in Column I names written on four ledger cards (lettered w, x, y, z) which have to be filed. You are to choose the option (lettered A, B, C, or D) in Column II which BEST represents the proper order for filing the cards.

SAMPLE

COLUMN I	COLUMN II
w. John Stevens	A. w, y, z, x
x. John D. Stevenson	B. y, w, z, x
y. Joan Stevens	C. x, y, w, z
z. J. Stevenson	D. x, w, y, z

The correct way to file the cards is:
y. Joan Stevens
w. John Stevens
z. J. Stevenson
x. John D. Stevenson

The correct order is shown by the letters y, w, z, x in that sequence. Since, in Column II, B appears in front of the letters y, w, z, x in that sequence, B is the correct answer to the sample question.

Now answer the following questions, using the same procedure.

9. COLUMN I
w. Juan Montoya
x. Manuel Montenegro
y. Victor Matos
z. Victoria Maltos

COLUMN II
A. y, z, x, w
B. z, y, x, w
C. z, y, w, x
D. y, x, z, w

9.____

10. COLUMN I
w. Frank Carlson
x. Robert Carlson
y. George Carlson
z. Frank Carlton

COLUMN II
A. z, x, w, y
B. z, y, x, w
C. w, y, z, x
D. w, z, y, x

10.____

11. COLUMN I
w. Carmine Rivera
x. Jose Rivera
y. Frank River
z. Joan Rivers

COLUMN II
A. y, w, x, z
B. y, x, w, z
C. w, x, y, z
D. w, x, z, y

11.____

12. COLUMN I
w. Jerome Mathews
x. Scott A. Matthew
y. Charles B. Matthew
z. Scott C. Mathewsw

COLUMN II
A. w, y, z, x
B. z, y, x, w
C. z, w, x, y
D. w, z, y, x

12.____

13. COLUMN I
w. John McMahan
x. John P. MacMahan
y. Joseph DeMayo
z. Joseph D. Mayo

COLUMN II
A. w, x, y, z
B. y, x, z, w
C. x, w, y, z
D. y, x, w, z

13.____

14. COLUMN I
w. Raymond Martinez
x. Ramon Martinez
y. Prof. Ray Martinez
z. Dr. Raymond Martin

COLUMN II
A. z, x, y, w
B. z, y, x, w
C. z, w, y, x
D. y, x, w, z

14.____

15. COLUMN I
w. Mr. Robert Vincent Mackintosh
x. Robert Reginald Macintosh
y. Roger V. McIntosh
z. Robert R. Mackintosh

COLUMN II
A. y, x, z, w
B. x, w, z, y
C. x, w, y, z
D. x, z, w, y

15.____

16. COLUMN I
w. Dr. D. V. Facsone
x. Prof. David Fascone
y. Donald Facsone
z. Mrs. D. Fascone

COLUMN II
A. y, w, z, x
B. w, y, x, z
C. w, y, z, x
D. z, w, x, y

16.____

17. COLUMN I
w. Johnathan Q. Addams
x. John Quincy Adams
y. J. Quincy Addams
z. Jerimiah Adams

COLUMN II
A. z, x, w, y
B. z, x, y, w
C. y, w, x, z
D. x, w, z, y

17.____

18. COLUMN I
w. Nehimiah Persoff
x. Newton Pershing
y. Newman Perring
z. Nelson Persons

COLUMN II
A. w, z, x, y
B. x, z, y, w
C. y, x, w, z
D. z, y, w, x

18.____

KEY (CORRECT ANSWERS)

1.	A	6.	D	11.	A	16.	C
2.	D	7.	D	12.	D	17.	B
3.	B	8.	C	13.	B	18.	C
4.	D	9.	B	14.	A		
5.	C	10.	C	15.	D		

TEST 4

Questions 1-13.

DIRECTIONS: Each question from 1 through 13 contains four names. For each question, choose the name that should be FIRST if he four names are to be arranged in alphabetical order in accordance with the Rule for Alphabetical Filing of Names of People given below. Read this rule carefully. Then, for each question, mark your answer space with the letter that is next to the name that should be first in alphabetical order.

RULE FOR ALPHABETICAL FILING OF NAMES OF PEOPLE

The names of people are filed in strict alphabetical order, first according to the last name, then according to the first name. For example; George Allen comes before Edward Bell, and Alice Reston comes before Lucille Reston.

SAMPLE QUESTION

A. Roger Smith (2)
B. Joan Smythe (4)
C. Alan Smith (1)
D. James Smithe (3)

The number in parentheses show the proper alphabetical order in which these names should be filed. Since the name that should be filed FIRST is Alan Smith, the correct answer to the sample question is C.

1. A. William Claremont B. Antonio Clements 1.____
C. Anthony Clemente D. William Claymont

2. A. Wayne Fumando B. Sarah Femando 2.____
C. Susan Fumando D. Wilson Femando

3. A. Wilbur Hanson B. Wm. Hansen 3.____
C. Robert Hansen D. Thomas Hanson

4. A. George St. John B. Thomas Santos 4.____
C. Frances Starks D. Mary S. Stranum

5. A. Franklin Carrol B. Timothy Carrol 5.____
C. Timothy S. Carol D. Frank F. Carroll

6. A. Christie-Barry Storage B. John Christie-Barry 6.____
C. The Christie-Barry Company D. Anne Christie-Barrie

7. A. Inter State Travel Co. A. Interstate Car Rental 7.____
C. Inter State Trucking D. Interstate Lending Inst.

8. A. The Los Angeles Tile Co. 8.____
   B. Anita F. Los
   C. The Lost & Found Detective Agency
   D. Jason Los-Brio

9. A. Prince Charles B. Prince Charles Coiffures 9.____
   C. Chas. F. Prince D. Thomas A. Charles

10. A. U.S. Dept. of Agriculture B. United States Aircraft Co. 10.____
    C. U.S. Air Transport, Inc. D. The United Union

11. A. Meyer's Art Shop B. Frank B. Meyer 11.____
    C. Meyers' Paint Store D. Meyer and Goldberg

12. A. David Des Laurier B. Des Moines Flower Shop 12.____
    C. Henry Desanto D. Mary L. Desta

13. A. Jeffrey Van Der Meer B. Jeffrey M. Vander 13.____
    C. Jeffrey Van D. Wallace Meer

KEY (CORRECT ANSWERS)

1.	A	6.	D	11.	A
2.	B	7.	B	12.	C
3.	C	8.	B	13.	D
4.	A	9.	D		
5.	C	10.	C		

TEST 5

Questions 1-10.

DIRECTIONS: Questions 1 through 10 are to be answered on the basis of the usual rules of filing. Column I lists, next to the numbers 1 to 10, the names of 10 clinic patients. Column II lists, next to the letters A to D, the headings of file drawers into which you are to place the records of these patients. For each question, indicate in the space at the right the letter preceding the heading of the file drawer in which the record should be filed.

	COLUMN I	COLUMN II	
1.	Charles Coughlin	A. Cab-Cep	1.____
2.	Mary Carstairs	B. Ceq-Cho	2.____
3.	Joseph Collin	C. Chr-Coj	3.____
4.	Thomas Chelsey	D. Cok-Czy	4.____
5.	Cedric Chalmers		5.____
6.	Mae Clarke		6.____
7.	Dora Copperhead		7.____
8.	Arnold Cohn		8.____
9.	Charlotte Crumboldt		9.____
10.	Frances Celine		10.____

Questions 11-18.

DIRECTIONS: Questions 11 to 18 are to be answered on the basis of the usual rules of filing. Column I lists, next to the numbers 11 to 18, the names of 8 clinic patients. Column II lists, next to the letters A to O, the headings of file drawers into which you are to place the records of these patients. For each question, indicate in the space at the right the letter preceding the heading of the file drawer in which the record should be filed.

COLUMN I	COLUMN II	
11. Thomas Adams	A. Aab-Abi	11.____
	B. Abj-Ach	
12. Joseph Albert	C. Aci-Aco	12.____
	D. Acp-Ada	
13. Frank Anaster	E. Adb-Afr	13.____
	F. Afs-Ago	
14. Charles Abt	G. Agp-Ahz	14.____
	H. Aia-Ako	
15. John Alfred	I. Akp-Ald	15.____
	J. Ale-Amo	
16. Louis Aron	K. Amp-Aor	16.____
	L. Aos-Apr	
17. Francis Amos	M. Aps-Asi	17.____
	N. Asj-Ati	
18. William Adler	O. Atj-Awz	18.____

Questions 19-28.

DIRECTIONS: Questions 19 through 28 are to be answered on the basis of the usual rules of filing. Column I lists, next to the numbers 19 through 28, the names of 10 clinic patients. Column II lists, next to the letters A to D the headings of file drawers into which you are to place the medical records of these patients. For each question, indicate in the space at the right the letter preceding the heading of the file drawer in which the record should be filed.

COLUMN I	COLUMN II	
19. Frank Shea	A. Sab-Sej	19.____
20. Rose Seaborn	B. Sek-Sio	20.____
21. Samuel Smollin	C. Sip-Soo	21.____
22. Thomas Shur	D. Sop-Syz	22.____
23. Ben Schaefer		23.____
24. Shirley Strauss		24.____
25. Harry Spiro		25.____
26. Dora Skelly		26.____
27. Sylvia Smith		27.____
28. Arnold Selz		28.____

KEY (CORRECT ANSWERS)

1.	D	11.	D	21.	C
2.	A	12.	I	22.	B
3.	D	13.	K	23.	A
4.	B	14.	B	24.	D
5.	B	15.	J	25.	D
6.	C	16.	M	26.	C
7.	D	17.	J	27.	C
8.	C	18.	E	28.	B
9.	D	19.	B		
10.	A	20.	A		

INTERPRETING STATISTICAL DATA GRAPHS, CHARTS AND TABLES

EXAMINATION SECTION

TEST 1

DIRECTIONS: Each question or incomplete statement is followed by several suggested answers or completions. Select the one that BEST answers the question or completes the statement. *PRINT THE LETTER OF THE CORRECT ANSWER IN THE SPACE AT THE RIGHT.*

Questions 1-8.

DIRECTIONS: Questions 1 through 8 are to be answered SOLELY on the basis of the information and chart given below.

The following chart shows expenses in five selected categories for a one-year period expressed as percentages of these same expenses during the previous year. The chart compares two different offices. In Office T (represented by ) a cost reduction program has been tested for the past year. The other office, Office Q (represented by ) served as a control, in that no special effort was made to reduce costs during the past year.

RESULTS OF OFFICE COST REDUCTION PROGRAM

Expenses of Test and Control Groups for 2019
Expressed as Percentages of Same Expenses for 2018

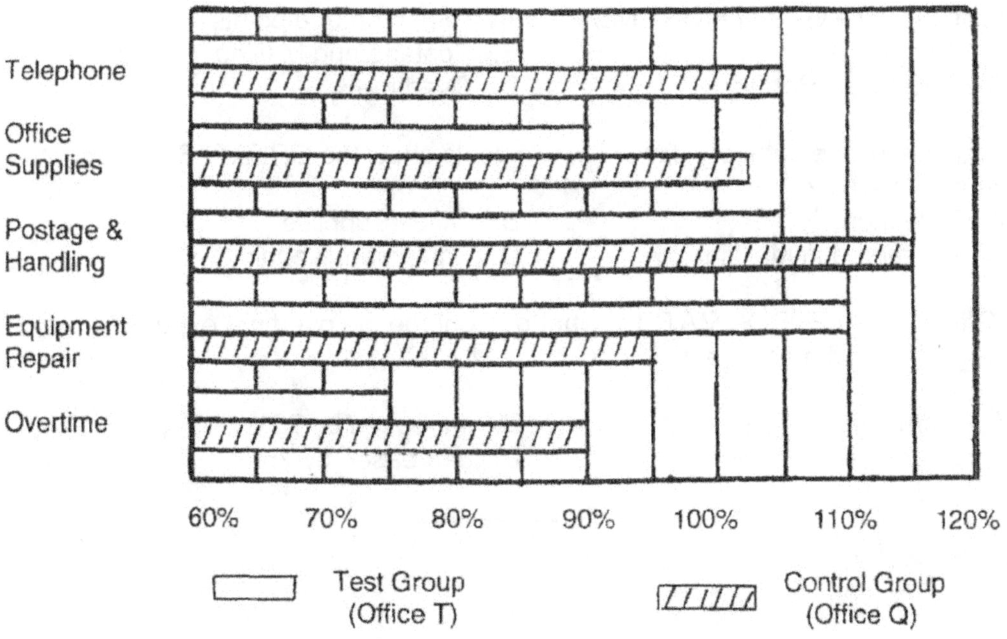

1. In Office T, which category of expenses showed the GREATEST percentage reduction from 2018 to 2019? 1.____
   A. Telephone B. Office Supplies
   C. Postage and Mailing D. Overtime

2. In which expense category did Office T show the BEST results in percentage terms when compared to Office Q? 2.____
   A. Telephone B. Office Supplies
   C. Postage and Mailing D. Overtime

3. According to the above chart, the cost reduction program was LEAST effective for the expense category of 3.____
   A. Office Supplies B. Postage and Mailing
   C. Equipment Repair D. Overtime

4. Office T's telephone costs went down during 2019 by APPROXIMATELY how many percentage points? 4.____
   A. 15 B. 20 C. 85 D. 105

5. Which of the following changes occurred in expenses for Office Supplies in Office Q in the year 2019 as compared with the year 2018? 5.____
   They
   A. *increased* by more than 100%
   B. *remained* the same
   C. *decreased* by a few percentage points
   D. *increased* by a few percentage points

6. For which of the following expense categories do the results in Office T and the results in Office Q differ MOST NEARLY by 10 percentage points? 6.____
   A. Telephone B. Postage and Mailing
   C. Equipment Repair D. Overtime

7. In which expense category did Office Q's costs show the GREATEST percentage increase in 2019? 7.____
   A. Telephone B. Office Supplies
   C. Postage and Mailing D. Equipment Repair

8. In Office T, by APPROXIMATELY what percentage did overtime expense change during the past year? 8.____
   It
   A. *increased* by 15% B. *increased* by 75%
   C. *decreased* by 10% D. *decreased* by 25%

KEY (CORRECT ANSWERS)

1.	D	5.	D
2.	A	6.	B
3.	C	7.	C
4.	A	8.	D

TEST 2

DIRECTIONS: Each question or incomplete statement is followed by several suggested answers or completions. Select the one that BEST answers the question or completes the statement. *PRINT THE LETTER OF THE CORRECT ANSWER IN THE SPACE AT THE RIGHT.*

Questions 1-7.

DIRECTIONS: Questions 1 through 7 are to be answered SOLELY on the basis of the information contained in the following graph which relates to the work of a public agency.

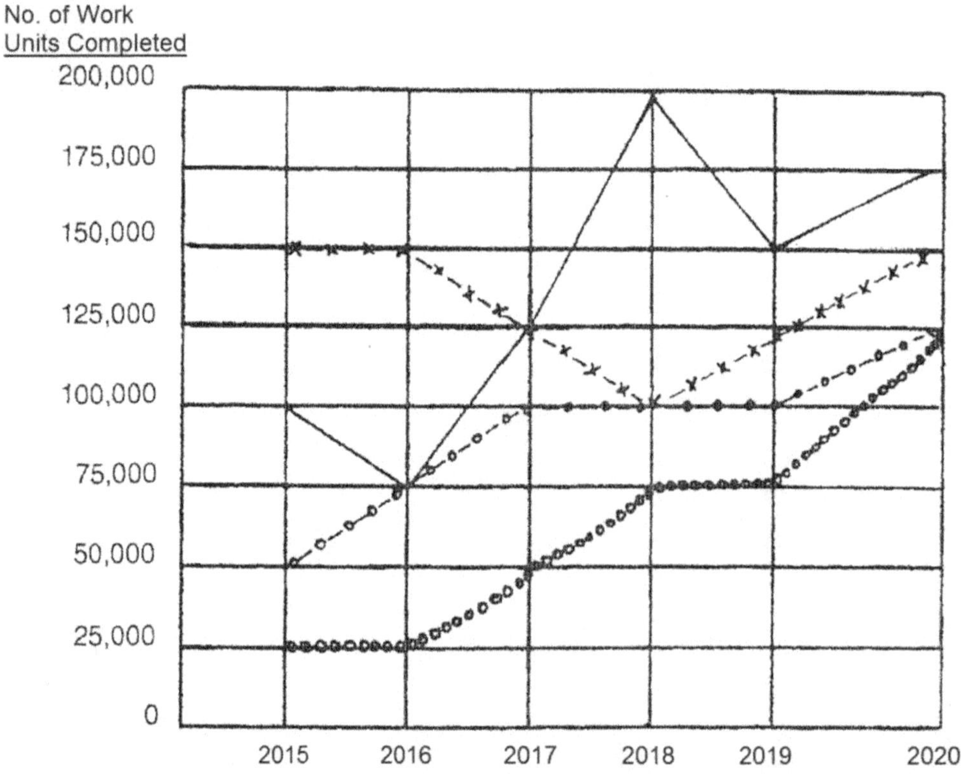

Units of each type of work completed by a public agency from 2015 to 2020.

Letters Written ————
Documents Filed –x-x-x-x-x-x-x
Applications Processed -0-0-0-0-0
Inspections Made 0000000000000

1. The year for which the number of units of one type of work completed was less than it was for the previous year while the number of each of the other types of work completed was more than it was for the previous year was 1.____
   A. 2016 B. 2017 C. 2018 D. 2019

2. The number of letters written exceeded the number of applications processed by the same amount in _____ of the years. 2.____
   A. two B. three C. four D. five

3. The year in which the number of each type of work completed was GREATER than in the preceding year was 3.____
   A. 2017 B. 2018 C. 2019 D. 2020

4. The number of applications processed and the number of documents filed were the SAME in 4.____
   A. 2016 B. 2017 C. 2018 D. 2019

5. The TOTAL number of units of work completed by the agency 5.____
   A. increased in each year after 2015
   B. decreased from the prior year in two of the years after 2015
   C. was the same in two successive years from 2015 to 2020
   D. was less in 2015 than in any of the following years

6. For the year in which the number of letters written was twice as high as it was in 2015, the number of documents filed was _____ it was in 2015. 6.____
   A. the same as
   B. two-thirds of what
   C. five-sixths of what
   D. one and one-half times what

7. The variable which was the MOST stable during the period 2015 through 2020 was 7.____
   A. Inspections Made
   B. Letters Written
   C. Documents Filed
   D. Applications Processed

KEY (CORRECT ANSWERS)

1.	B	5.	C
2.	B	6.	B
3.	D	7.	D
4.	C		

TEST 3

DIRECTIONS: Each question or incomplete statement is followed by several suggested answers or completions. Select the one that BEST answers the question or completes the statement. *PRINT THE LETTER OF THE CORRECT ANSWER IN THE SPACE AT THE RIGHT.*

Questions 1-10.

DIRECTIONS: Questions 1 through 10 are to be answered SOLELY on the basis of the REPORT OF TELEPHONE CALLS table given below.

TABLE – REPORT OF TELEPHONE CALLS

Dept.	No. of Stations	No. of Employees	No. of Incoming Calls In		No. of Long Distance Calls in		No. of Divisions
			2019	2020	2019	2020	
I	11	40	3421	4292	72	54	5
II	36	330	10392	10191	75	78	18
III	53	250	85243	85084	103	98	8
IV	24	60	9675	10123	82	85	6
V	13	30	5208	5492	54	48	6
VI	25	35	7472	8109	86	90	5
VII	37	195	11412	11299	68	72	11
VIII	36	54	8467	8674	59	68	4
IX	163	306	294321	289968	289	321	13
X	40	83	9588	8266	93	89	5
XI	24	68	7867	7433	86	87	13
XII	50	248	10039	10208	101	95	30
XIII	10	230	7550	6941	28	21	10
XVI	25	103	14281	14392	48	40	5
XV	19	230	8475	206	38	43	8
XVI	22	45	4684	5584	39	48	10
XVII	41	58	10102	9677	49	52	6
XVIII	82	106	106242	105889	128	132	10
XIX	6	13	2649	2498	35	29	2
XX	16	30	1395	1468	78	90	2

1. The department which had more than 106,000 incoming calls in 2019 but fewer than 250,000 is 1.____
   A. II B. IX C. XVIII D. III

2. The department which has fewer than 8 divisions and more than 100 but fewer than 300 employees is 2.____
   A. VII B. XIV C. XV D. XVIII

3. The department which had an increase in 2020 over 2019 in the number of both incoming and long distance calls but had an increase in long distance calls of not more than 3 was 3.____
   A. IV B. VI C. XVII D. XVIII

4. The department which had a decrease in the number of incoming calls in 2020 as compared to 2019 and has not less than 6 nor more than 7 divisions is 4.____
   A. IV B. V C. XVII D. III

5. The department which has more than 7 divisions and more than 200 employees but fewer than 19 stations is 5.____
   A. XV B. III C. XX D. XIII

6. The department having more than 10 divisions and fewer than 36 stations, which had an increase in long distance calls in 2020 over 2019, is 6.____
   A. XI B. VII C. XVI D. XVIII

7. The department which in 2020 had at least 7,250 incoming calls and a decrease in long distance calls from 2019 and has more than 50 stations is 7.____
   A. IX B. XII C. XVIII D. III

8. The department which has fewer than 25 stations, fewer than 100 employees, 10 or more divisions, and showed an increase of at least 9 long distance calls in 2020 over 2019 is 8.____
   A. IX B. XVI C. XX D. XIII

9. The department which has more than 50 but fewer than 125 employees and had more than 5,000 incoming calls in 2019 but not more than 10,000, and more than 60 long distance calls in 2020 but not more than 85, and has more than 24 stations is 9.____
   A. VIII B. XIV C. IV D. XI

10. If the number of departments showing an increase in long distance calls in 2020 over 1999 exceeds the number showing a decrease in long distance calls in the same period, select the Roman numeral indicating the department having less than one station for each 10 employees, provided not more than 8 divisions are served by that department. 10.____
    If the number of departments showing an increase in long distance calls in 2020 over 2019 does not exceed the number showing a decrease in long distance calls in the same period, select the Roman numeral indicating the department having the SMALLEST number of incoming calls in 2020.
    A. III B. XIII C. XV D. XX

KEY (CORRECT ANSWERS)

1.	C	6.	A
2.	B	7.	D
3.	A	8.	B
4.	C	9.	A
5.	D	10.	C

TEST 4

DIRECTIONS: Each question or incomplete statement is followed by several suggested answers or completions. Select the one that BEST answers the question or completes the statement. *PRINT THE LETTER OF THE CORRECT ANSWER IN THE SPACE AT THE RIGHT.*

Questions 1-6.

DIRECTIONS: Questions 1 through 6 are to be answered SOLELY on the basis of the information given in the following chart. This chart shows the results of a study made of the tasks performed by a stenographer during one day. Included in the chart are the time at which she started a certain task and, under the particular heading, the amount of time, in minutes, she took to complete the task, and explanations of telephone calls and miscellaneous activities.
NOTE: The time spent at lunch should not be included in any of your calculations.

PAMELA JOB STUDY

NAME: Pamela Donald — DATE: 9/26
JOB TITLE: Stenographer
DIVISION: Stenographic Pool

Time of Start of Task	TASKS PERFORMED						Explanations of Telephone Calls and Miscellaneous Activities
	Taking Dictation	Typing	Filing	Telephone Work	Handling Mail	Misc. Activities	
9:00					22		
9:22						13	Picking up supplies
9:35						15	Cleaning typewriter
9:50	11						
10:01		30					
10:31				8			Call to Agency A
10:39	12						
10:51			10				
11:01				7			Call from Agency B
11:08		30					
11:38	10						
11:48				12			Call from Agency C
12:00	L U N C H						
1:00					28		
1:28	13						
1:41-2:13		32		12			Call to Agency B
X			15				
Y		50					
3:30	10						
3:40			21				
4:01				9			Call from Agency A
4:10	35						
4:45		9					
4:54						6	Cleaning up desk

SAMPLE QUESTION:
The total amount of time spent on miscellaneous activities in the morning is exactly equal to the total amount of time spent

A. filing in the morning
B. handling mail in the afternoon
C. miscellaneous activities in the afternoon
D. handling mail in the morning

Explanation of answer to sample question:
The total amount of time spent on miscellaneous activities in the morning equals 28 minutes (13 minutes for picking up supplies plus 15 minutes for cleaning the typewriter); and since it takes 28 minutes to handle mail in the afternoon, the answer is B.

1. The time labeled Y at which the stenographer started a typing assignment was 1.____

A. 2:15 B. 2:25 C. 2:40 D. 2:50

2. The ratio of time spent on all incoming calls to time spent on all outgoing calls for the day was 2.____

A. 5:7 B. 5:12 C. 7:5 D. 7:12

3. Of the following combinations of tasks, which ones take up exactly 80% of the total time spent on Tasks Performed during the day? 3.____

A. Typing, Filing, Telephone Work, Handling Mail
B. Taking Dictation, Filing, and Miscellaneous Activities
C. Taking Dictation, Typing, Handling Mail, and Miscellaneous Activities
D. Taking Dictation, Typing, Filing, and Telephone Work

4. The total amount of time spent transcribing or typing work is how much MORE than the total amount of time spent in taking dictation? 4.____

A. 55 minutes B. 1 hour
C. 1 hour 10 minutes D. 1 hour 25 minutes

5. The GREATEST number of shifts in activities occurred between the times of 5.____

A. 9:00 A.M. and 10:31 A.M. B. 9:35 A.M. and 11:01 A.M.
C. 10:31 A.M. and 12:00 Noon D. 3:30 P.M. and 5:00 P.M.

6. The total amount of time spent on Taking Dictation in the morning plus the total amount of time spent on Filing in the afternoon is exactly EQUAL to the total amount of time spent on 6.____

A. Typing in the afternoon minus the total amount of time spent on Telephone Work in the afternoon
B. Typing in the morning plus the total amount of time spent on Miscellaneous Activities
C. Dictation in the afternoon plus the total amount of time spent on Filing in the morning
D. Typing in the afternoon minus the total amount of time spent in Handling Mail in the morning

KEY (CORRECT ANSWERS)

1. C
2. C
3. D
4. B
5. C
6. D

TEST 5

DIRECTIONS: Each question or incomplete statement is followed by several suggested answers or completions. Select the one that BEST answers the question or completes the statement. *PRINT THE LETTER OF THE CORRECT ANSWER IN THE SPACE AT THE RIGHT.*

Questions 1-8.

DIRECTIONS: Questions 1 through 8 are to be answered SOLELY on the basis of the information given in the following table.

	Bronx		Brooklyn		Manhattan		Queens		Richmond	
	May	June	May	June	May	June	May	June	May	June
Number of Clerks in Office Assigned To Issue Applications for Licenses	3	4	6	8	6	8	3	5	2	4
Number of Licenses Issued	950	1010	1620	1940	1705	2025	895	1250	685	975
Amount Collected in License Fees	$42,400	$52,100	$77,600	$94,500	$83,700	$98,800	$39,300	$65,500	$30,600	$48,200
Number of Inspectors	4	5	6	7	7	8	4	5	2	4
Number of Inspections Made	420	450	630	710	690	740	400	580	320	440
Number of Violations Found As a Result of Inspections	211	153	352	378	320	385	256	304	105	247

1. Of the following statements, the one which is NOT accurate on the basis of an inspection of the information contained in the table is that, for each office, the increase from May to June in the number of 1.____
   A. inspectors was accompanied by an increase in the number of inspections made
   B. licenses issued was accompanied by an increase in the amount collected in license fees
   C. inspections made was accompanied by an increase in the number of violations found
   D. licenses issued was accompanied by an increase in the number of clerks assigned to issue applications for licenses

2. The TOTAL number of licenses issued by all five offices in the Division in May was 2.____
   A. 4,800 B. 5,855 C. 6,865 D. 7,200

3. The total number of inspectors in all five borough offices in June exceeded the number in May by MOST NEARLY 3.____
   A. 21% B. 26% C. 55% D. 70%

4. In the month of June, the number of violations found per inspection made was the HIGHEST in 4.____
   A. Brooklyn B. Manhattan C. Queens D. Richmond

5. In the month of May, the average number of inspections made by an inspector in the Bronx was the same as the average number of inspections made by an inspector in 5.____
   A. Brooklyn B. Manhattan C. Queens D. Richmond

6. Assume that in June all of the inspectors in the Division spent 7 hours a day making inspections on each of the 21 working days in the month. 6.____
   Then the average amount of time that an inspector in the Manhattan office spent on an inspection that month was MOST NEARLY
   A. 2 hours
   B. 1 hour and 35 minutes
   C. 1 hour and 3 minutes
   D. 38 minutes

7. If an average fine of $100 was imposed for a violation found by the Division, what was the TOTAL amount in fines imposed for all the violations found by the Division in May? 7.____
   A. $124,400 B. $133,500 C. $146,700 D. $267,000

8. Assume that the amount collected in license fees by the entire Division in May was 80 percent of the amount collected by the entire Division in April. 8.____
   How much was collected by the entire Division in April?
   A. $218,880 B. $328,320 C. $342,000 D. $410,400

KEY (CORRECT ANSWERS)

1.	C	5.	A
2.	B	6.	B
3.	B	7.	A
4.	D	8.	C

TEST 6

DIRECTIONS: Each question or incomplete statement is followed by several suggested answers or completions. Select the one that BEST answers the question or completes the statement. *PRINT THE LETTER OF THE CORRECT ANSWER IN THE SPACE AT THE RIGHT.*

Questions 1-8.

DIRECTIONS: Questions 1 through 8 are to be answered SOLELY on the basis of the information contained in the chart and table shown below, which relate to Bureau X in a certain public agency. The chart shows the percentage of the bureau's annual expenditures spent on equipment, supplies, and salaries for each of the years 2016-2020. The table shows the bureau's annual expenditures for each of the years 2016-2020.

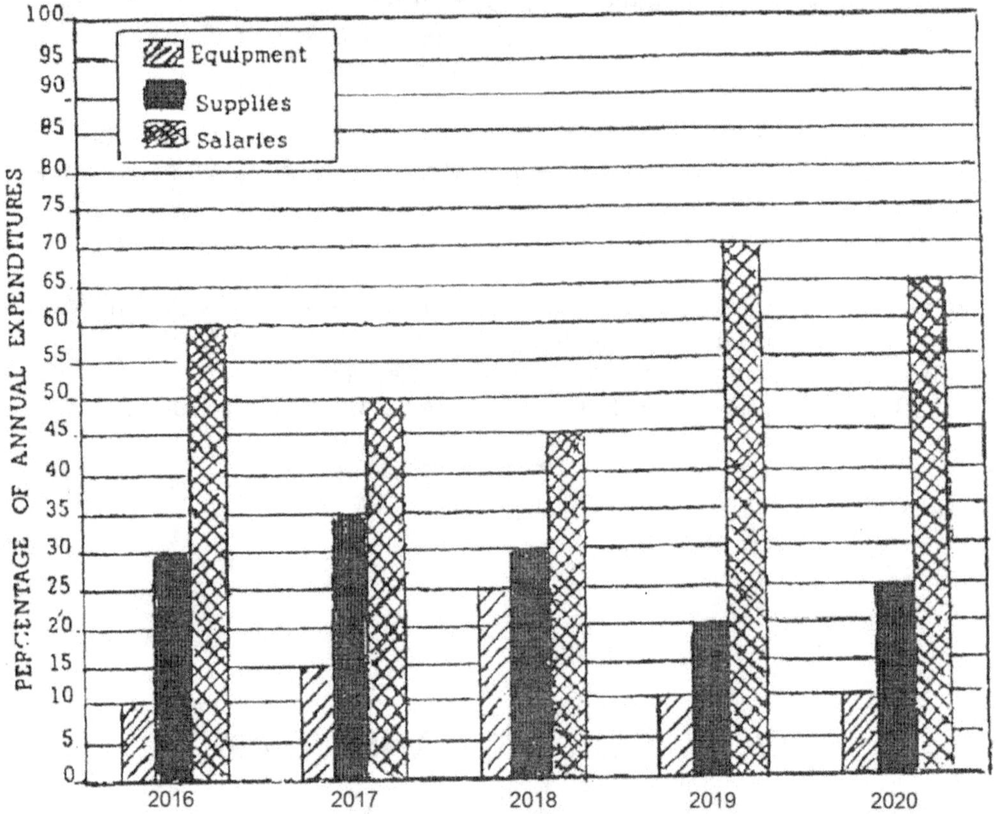

The bureau's annual expenditures for the years 2016-2020 are shown in the following table:

YEAR	EXPENDITURES
2016	$8,000,000
2017	$12,000,000
2018	$15,000,000
2019	$10,000,000
2020	$12,000,000

Equipment, supplies, and salaries were the only three categories for which the bureau spent money.

Candidates may find it useful to arrange their computations on their scratch paper in an orderly manner since the correct computations for one question may also be helpful in answering another question.

1. The information contained in the chart and table is sufficient to determine the 1.____
   A. average annual salary of an employee in the bureau in 2017
   B. decrease in the amount of money spent on supplies in the bureau in 2016 from the amount spent in the preceding year
   C. changes between 2018 and 2019 in the prices of supplies bought by the bureau
   D. increase in the amount of money spent on salaries in the bureau in 2020 over the amount spent in the preceding year

2. If the percentage of expenditures for salaries in one year is added to the percentage of expenditures for equipment in that year, a total of two percentages for that year is obtained. 2.____
   The two years for which this total is the SAME are
   A. 2016 and 2018
   B. 2017 and 2019
   C. 2016 and 2019
   D. 2017 and 2020

3. Of the following, the year in which the bureau spent the GREATEST amount of money on supplies was 3.____
   A. 2020 B. 2018 C. 2016 D. 2016

4. Of the following years, the one in which there was the GREATEST increase over the preceding year in the amount of money spent on salaries is 4.____
   A. 2019 B. 2020 C. 2016 D. 2018

5. Of the bureau's expenditures for equipment in 2020, one-third was used for the purchase of mailroom equipment and the remainder was spent on miscellaneous office equipment. 5.____
   How much did the bureau spend on miscellaneous office equipment in 2020?
   A. $4,000,000 B. $400,000 C. $8,000,000 D. $800,000

6. If there were 120 employees in the bureau in 2019, then the average annual salary paid to the employees in that year was MOST NEARLY 6.____
   A. $43,450 B. $49,600 C. $58,350 D. $80,800

7. In 2018, the bureau had 125 employees. 7.____
   If 20 of the employees earned an average annual salary of $80,000, then the average salary of the other 105 employees was MOST NEARLY
   A. $49,000 B. $64,000 C. $41,000 D. $54,000

8. Assume that the bureau estimated that the amount of money it would spend on supplies in 2021 would be the same as the amount it spent on that category in 2020. Similarly, the bureau estimated that the amount of money it would spend on equipment in 2021 would be the same as the amount it spent on that category in 2020. However, the bureau estimated that in 2021 the amount it would spend on salaries would be 10 percent higher than the amount it spent on that category in 2020. 8.____
The percentage of its annual expenditures that the bureau estimated it would spend on supplies in 2021 is MOST NEARLY
A. 27.5% B. 23.5% C. 22.5% D. 25%

KEY (CORRECT ANSWERS)

1.	D	5.	D
2.	A	6.	C
3.	B	7.	A
4.	C	8.	B

---

www.ingramcontent.com/pod-product-compliance
Lightning Source LLC
Chambersburg PA
CBHW080742250426
43671CB00038B/2837
* 9 7 8 1 7 9 9 3 6 7 6 0 4 *